SCHOOLIN'S LOG

SCHOOLIN'S LOG
Llewelyn Jones

Illustrations by Derek Crowe

MICHAEL JOSEPH LONDON

First published in Great Britain by
Michael Joseph Limited
44 Bedford Square, London W.C.1.
1980

Text © 1980 by Llewelyn Jones
Illustrations © 1980 by Derek Crowe

ISBN 0 7181 1849 9

Printed in Great Britain by
Hollen Street Press Ltd. Slough, Berkshire
and bound by Hunter and Foulis Ltd. Edinburgh

For my children Penny Myfanwy and Andrew

PARISH OF ST NICHOLAS

ADMINISTRATIVE COUNTY OF PEMBROKE

Area   = *2,182 acres*
Number of persons   =   *205 (90 males and 115 females)*
Number of households   =   *46*
Number of persons per acre =   *0.1*

From: *Census of England and Wales 1921*

This is an account of life between the two world wars in the North Pembrokeshire village of St Nicholas where the author's father was schoolmaster. The verbatim reports are taken from the Headmaster's Log, the Minute Book of the School Managers, and the Minutes of the St Nicholas Parish Council.

The events described happened a long time ago, and memory is fallible, so the names have been changed except for those which figure in historical references.

CONTENTS

CHAPTER ONE

The Song of the Three R's

'It was proposed and passed unanimously that Mr J. Ll. Jones be appointed Head Teacher of the School and the Chairman promised to write, offering him the post.'

School Managers' Minutes, 9 June 1922

When Jack Jones the schoolmaster, known to everybody as Schoolin, opened the school door that autumn morning, a tide of hot gaseous air flooded his nose.

'Whew,' he breathed out gustily and made for the tall stove, on which a trio of molten tortoises were winking and pulsing round a slogan of 'Slow but Sure'.

He pushed in the floor damper, changing the roar of the stove to a loud whisper. He must warn poor old Mary Ann – the cleaner who lit the fire at seven o'clock – against wasting coal, which was already sky high at £2. 2s. 6d. a ton. The smell remained, and he opened the door and window to let in fresh air. At least the morning was fine, not like yesterday when steam from the children's soaked clothes, drying on the metal mesh stoveguard, had turned the big room into a laundry.

Schoolin unlocked his desk, took out the hazel cane which he had cut from the copse by Tresissillt river, laid two pieces of chalk in the groove specially provided and got out the Register. His gaze lingered a moment on the pictures and charts that draped and coloured the yellow distempered walls: African chiefs with David Livingstone; Children from Other Lands, looking like brightly attired dolls; six horses pulling a sail binder in a yellow Manitoba wheatfield; the Roll of Honour and above the clock, his own favourite picture of plover tumbling from a windy sky, with snow inside their wings.

He lifted the polished flap, reached out the heavy Log in which he entered up every morning at this time the previous day's Attendance and any unusual happening. Burly, medium height, with weather-beaten cheeks, myopic blue eyes, pince-nez and thick iron-grey hair, he was the least vain and ostentatious of men, but permitted himself one little Dickensian affectation each morning before the children arrived. He took lavish care and pride in his near copperplate handwriting – even on the blackboard on which

he chalked with wristy elegance – and he always wrote up the entries in his daily log with a quill, of which he saved a number each year from the three white geese he fattened for Christmas on the playing green.

Now he began to write, savouring the balance of the slowly moving tall plume.

'Owing to the thundery rain there were only 28 children present today. A terrific gale and torrential rain took place and at 3.30 p.m. Mr George of Trehilyn came with a market cart and reported the road flooded to a depth of 3ft at Ty-gwyn. All the children passing that way were taken in his cart to their home. The piano was tuned today by the County Council tuner.'

He closed the Log, flipped over the brass lock, and restored it, with the quill, to the niche in the desk.

The first children now began to arrive, headed by Hugh, the little cripple who dragged his clogged feet in semi-circles from the neighbouring hamlet, a mile away, and was never late; five children from Pen-y-Groet, all under sentence, though there was no hint of fate in their bright greetings on this autumn day; the three sisters who walked four miles each way from the tiny holding beneath the hill-fortress of Garn Fawr, who at the end of every

term took home the ornate Good Attendance Certificates signed by the vicar, which by now, almost papered their parlour walls.

As the cripple clumped and lumbered past, Schoolin reached out his hand and placed it gently on the boy's shoulder.

'Good boy, Hugh,' he said, 'always nice and early,' and received a carious smile of pleasure in return.

'Please, sir, can I be ink monitor today?'

Schoolin's light blue eyes moved to a burly boy with a shock of black hair and a flat face which descended without benefit of neck into a tieless celluloid collar, held with a golden stud, which had earned him the nickname of 'Collars' Morgan. The school day officially began as he answered, 'Yes, boy. The tea pot and ink

powder are in the cupboard. Mind to mix properly now. Not too pale. And don't overfill the inkwells. I'll tell you when to ring. Right, boy?' The accolyte nodded and departed, laden with responsibilities. His ink chore finished, he was then despatched to pull the kinky wire that rang the bell which, on winter nights when the gales roared in from the sea, addressed the sleeping village with carillons of its own.

St Nicholas school was a small, high granite building with steep gables and a blue slate roof, built in 1869, largely from parish subscriptions. (Before that date, the only source of education for the children of the parish was the Sunday School run by the nonconformist chapel.)

The school bell officially stopped ringing at 9.15 a.m., by which time the children were standing in the old teak desks, carved and chipped, and shiny from generations of patched elbows and corduroy bottoms. The older children occupied the desks nearest the windows under the weeping patch of damp (which like poor Mrs Magwen Morgan's ulcerated leg never dried summer or winter), flanked by the younger children in descending order down to the infants in the gangway.

Schoolin opened the oilcloth chart at 'Glory be to Jesus' and hung it on the blackboard and as his assistant Miss Prothero banged out the morning chords on the yellow notes of the newly-tuned piano, and the children began to sing, his eyes wandered over his brood, some patched and ragged, others neat as wrens. As he took in the infants to whose faces the morning hymn lent an earnest shine, Schoolin had to swallow his prominent Adam's apple and blink away a light mistiness which clouded his pince-nez. In forty years of teaching, the sight of toddlers singing the morning hymn never failed to move him.

The children recited the Lord's Prayer in Welsh and English –
Schoolin taught almost entirely in English though use of the
Pembrokeshire patois enabled pupils to have the best (or worst) of
both languages – and the moment had then arrived for the Register.
This was a large book with gold-scrolled red covers, which
contained in Schoolin's copperplate handwriting the names of the
fifty-three children at that time on the school roll. Those present
were marked in circles of black ink and the absentees in red circles
(a sort of nought out of ten mark).

Schoolin declaimed the names in ringing stentorian,
accompanying those of children from outlying areas with their
farms or cottages, in recognition of gallant distances walked.

'Mary Binyon, Banks Farm – present sir
Gwynfor Bowen, Ty Gwyn – present sir
Lilly Davies, Trefasser – present sir
Magwen Davies, Trefasser – present sir
Willie Evans – present, yes sir.'

This morning when the roll call reached 'David Jones,
Parsonage Farm' there was no reply.

'David Jones', the name was called again, and again receiving
no reply, the schoolmaster looked up and asked David's sister,
'Why is David away then, Ceinwen?'

'Please sir, he's very bad, our mam says he can't come this week.'

'What's the matter with him, then?'

Thirteen-year-old Ceinwen looked across at the boys, and said, with a slightly embarrassed air, 'Please sir, he can't stop going out the back . . .'

Delwyn Thomas, a neighbour of David, began to snigger and catching sight of his grimacing face, Schoolin shouted, – 'What are you grinning about there, you boy,' and restored wincing decorum with a thwack of his cane on the offender's shoulders, for bowels were respected by the schoolmaster as part of the recycling of Nature's fertility – and calling the Register was the most solemn business of the day.

Of the words that recur regularly in the Minutes of the School Managers and the Log Book kept by the headmaster over the years, 'Attendance' far outnumbers any other, because church schools were dependent on a good Register for their financial grants. When the number of pupils was particularly small, Schoolin crossed the road to the Oak Grange to consult with the Squire and to obtain formal permission to 'cancel the Register' for the day, so that the average percentage figure for the term did not suffer.

The two principal obstacles to a full school were the recurring bouts of illness – measles, influenza, whooping cough, diphtheria, typhoid, which sometimes closed the school for weeks on end – and the wet winters. On dark, rainy mornings with gales roaring in from the sea, it called for determined parents and children to undertake journeys down soaking pot-holed lanes, in some instances up to four miles each way and beginning with a walk across wet or flooded fields before the road proper began. So when the cracked bell was tinkled by the day's monitor on a stormy morning, the school might have village children only present. As the rain and gale pelted and buffeted the windows and the stove

roared its answers to the wind – and even occasionally blew open
with a crash so that belching smoke and flames licking into the
schoolroom brought the schoolmaster running to close it with the
long poker – the sense of holiday and cosiness grew in the Big
Room, until some of the more intrepid distant families began to
arrive, to hog the limelight. Stripped of sodden sacks and coats,
they were installed in grinning exclusivity round the stoveguard
where the tortoises received them with glowing fury.

But on this autumn morning, eighty-five percent of the children
had answered the roll call before Miss Prothero, tall, stooping,
grey-haired and grey-faced, led her ragged troupe of tinies through
the massive arched penetentiary-like door into the Little Room.

A few minutes later they could be heard chanting the St Nicholas
'Alphabet Song' in rhythmical groupings of letters:

abcdefg: hijklmnop: qrstuv: wxyz

It was chanting, chanting all the way to the Big Room, for
which the infants were given a simple test in the Three R's to
make sure they were ready. A backward child might spend a whole
year extra with Miss Prothero. It was Schoolin's belief that
young children absorbed facts more quickly (because more
enjoyably) when they sang them, and this was often borne out by
little groups of shrilling infants, singing their letters in the
playground in a sort of Ring-a-Roses game. (The echoes remained
even with adults who would realise, rather sheepishly, that they
were humming the St Nicholas 'Alphabet Song' in middle age.)
This rote and repetition technique was, for some unobvious reason,
particularly successful with infant religious instruction, and a
Diocesan Inspector's report in the Managers' Minutes testifies how
well the children had acquitted themselves, especially 'the Infants
Department (which) had shown a remarkable degree of intelligence'.
The whole school was examined annually in the Scriptures by the
Inspector who, for much of Schoolin's tenure, was a kindly elderly
clergyman, in whose face time seemed to stand still year after year.

The school was also visited by the County Director of Education
from Haverfordwest who always arrived unannounced, listened to

the teaching and sometimes set a test. He then submitted his judgement on the school to the Chairman of the Governors in the form of a Report, a word which had a special ring and meaning in the family discussions at School House. His Majesty's Inspector 'from London' also made a periodic fact-finding visit.

Throughout his long teaching career, Schoolin's overriding priority remained unchanged, which was to ensure that all his pupils should have a thorough grounding in the Three R's. At the close of his career, it was his proud claim that he could not recall one boy who had left his care without being able to read and write and do elementary arithmetic and if he married a Schoolin-educated wife, would also have a partner who could check bills, invoices and write his letters as well. Sums were always given the paramount place so that multiplication and the other arithmetical tables echoed at frequent regular intervals every day from the oak rafters of the Big Room. In summer especially, with the windows open, the recitations led by Schoolin's baritone and conducted with his hazel cane could be heard throughout the village. Nor did the schoolmaster give himself – any more than the children – a chance to forget at any time the supreme importance of tables, for cards of the multiplication tables, money, weight, lengths, capacity and time were attached with drawing pins to his hinged desk top, so that as the spirit moved him in the course of the day he could fire unexpected questions like bullets at the children.

This method of teaching facts – spelling especially was subject to the drumbeat system – brought its problems, especially in the Big Room where it often demanded adroit timetabling to avoid different groups reciting different messages in unison.

On this Monday morning, first freedom of the air belonged to the younger children but before he strode across the gangway to conduct their multiplication litany, Schoolin set work for the older pupils.

Often his teaching decisions were made on the spot and this morning he singled out a group of boys sitting together on the right of the gangway divide.

'Jimmy James, Llewelyn Jones, Gwyn Williams, Gwynfor Evans, Eddie Morgan, Delwyn Thomas, you boys, I want you to write a letter to the Prince of Wales. About catching moles. At least four lines. Best writing. And no lies now, mind.'

The Prince was a frequent letter-writing target of St Nicholas school, for Schoolin was greatly impressed by the future King's democratic touch which enabled him to consort with commoners

without dilution of dignity, (besides which he was personally
known to Major Willie Acraman, his wife Catherine's much
be-medalled Grenadier brother). To ensure that protocol was
properly observed, Schoolin wrote on the blackboard the correct
mode of address, 'May it please Your Royal Highness', the loyal
ending of 'I remain, Your Royal Highness's obedient Servant' and
the exciting destination of the missives: 'Buckingham Palace,
London, England'.

He turned to the older girls.

'You girls, open your poetry books at page 14. "The Brook" by
Alfred Lord Tennyson. First two verses.' (Tennyson and similar
titled personages always received their full titles which he
proclaimed with sonorous relish.)

'Copy these out as Penmanship. Careful there's no blots.
Remember to clean your nibs on your blotting paper and press
harder on the down strokes of the letters. If you finish, start
learning the first verse under your breath. Right?'

He moved to a group of boys. This was a quartet of high-flyers
soon to sit the scholarship examination for Fishguard County
School, which earned successful pupils £5 a year and a free place
and was very much the event by which the quality of the school
was judged by the parish, as well as by the bureaucrats. (Schoolin
was avidly alert to identify the potential bank clerk, vicar,
schoolmaster, minister and pass him or, rarely, her to the County
School. Over the years, pupils from the little village school entered
the Church, the professions of architect, banking, teaching,
educational administration and journalism.)

'Right,' said Schoolin, 'sums for you four. Take this down,' and
he began to improvise simple problems with a local colour.

'First.   If one and a half pounds of currants in Mr Bilbow's
           shop cost threepence farthing, work out the cost of
           one and a half hundredweights.

Second. If the price of vinegar in the shop is three and three
quarters pence a pint, work out the cost of twenty-seven
and two-thirds gallons, less three and seven-eighths
gallons.

Third. If all the lamps in St Nicholas use five and
seven-eighths pints of paraffin every six days, how much
will they use from October the thirty-first to March the
nineteenth inclusive?'

'Show your workings,' he said.

Schoolin then returned to the front of the class where he did a
little ritual walking up and down, shoulders slightly hunched,
addressing the pupils in the operatic semi-roar which he used on
such occasions, fixing them with his bright blue stare.

'Now children, get on with your work. If I find that anyone has
not been trying his best, he'll be for it. Right?' and with this, he
marched across to the younger children where the youthful monitor
for the day had set up the little blackboard.

Schoolin's voice was gentler as he addressed this small brood.
He singled out a black-jerseyed little boy with basin haircut.

'Well, Willie,' he said, 'how's that old bottom tooth then?' The
previous Friday he had been rubbing the area round the decaying
milk tooth with bicarbonate of soda. Willie – his son Llewelyn's
best friend – whose top gums were conspicuously empty except for
two stubborn sentinel canines which had earned him the nickname
of Tusks, provided his nearest equivalent of a smile.

Schoolin addressed the class.

'Now boys and girls, what are we on today, then? Nine times,
isn't it. Some of you are getting on quite nicely with your tables,
you know, and I shall tell your fathers and mothers about you
when I see them. But some of you will have to pay more attention
and try much harder, won't you? Now where is the nine times
table?'

He sorted the day's table from the group of heavily printed

oilcloth sheets, rolled on a round pole at one end, and hung it over the blackboard.

For a whole half hour of shrill repetition the children lived with the nine times table. From time to time, to prevent boredom Schoolin rang the changes, calling out lines in varying sequences.

Then the command came, 'Now close your eyes. Bronwen, what are five nines ?'

'Forty-five, sir'

'Is she right, children ? All together now.'

He left them with the task of copying out the table in best writing, and returned to the older children. One of the correspondents was still writing to the Prince, for while moles were a happy choice of subject for Jimmy James, a smiling brown-eyed bullet-headed boy with close-cropped hair, a low brow and stained teeth, the three R's never produced his finest hour. He gave out an aura of sweat and corduroy and was Schoolin's son's desk mate. Yet while Jimmy's mind remained confused about poles, perches and gills (which he tended to get mixed up with horses, poultry and fish anyhow), he was a deadly killer of the little velvet-jacketed miners who tunnelled and heaved beneath the stony St Nicholas fields, and he despatched regular consignments of cured glossy skins to John Lee of Birmingham whose moleskin prices were his constant topic of conversation. So it was not surprising that Jimmy was last to finish. He put down his pen with a sigh and began to bite his nails. Schoolin chose his son to read out the first letter.

Llewelyn stood up, heart-faced, long-necked, thin, shy, heart pounding and yet excited at the prospect. His letter revealed his love of big show-off words.

'Moles', he read, 'are subterranean animals which means they live underground. They make elongated tunnels with their noses and feet. They show as molehills, hence the saying making mountains out of molehills. Their fur is very warm and insulates them from the cold. They are caught in traps.'

'That's quite good, Llewelyn,' said his father, hiding a smile at the big words, conscious his son was not quite ten years old.

Jimmy's letter, as befitted a specialist, was more down to earth, with nuggets of real information,

'Moles', Jimmy wrote to the heir of the throne, 'is a dammo noosence in fields. But I loves em. I sets in their tewnells before I comes to school and wer gluves to mak sure my stink not make them run away. Hopes you are the same. Your obedient sarvint. James james. I traps the little buggers and sells em to Jon Lee.'

The noun in the last sentence produced titters and Schoolin, himself failing to control a small grin, expostulated. 'Beggars, Jimmy, beggars,' and he spelled out 'beggars' in a loud voice.

Gwyn Williams earned approval for his assurance to the Prince that His Royal Highness could trap moles on Trevayog Farm any time he happened to visit the area, while Gwynfor, the rabbit trapper's son, made contemptuous reference to the mole which was blind and could be neither stewed, roasted nor made into pies. Having checked the spelling and ordered Llewelyn to help Jimmy rewrite his letter with correct spelling, Schoolin then examined the girls' penmanship, marked the sums, and it was playtime.

Built on common land which remained unfenced, the St Nicholas school playground ran into the surrounding countryside which, during school hours, was a rich source of digressions, always welcome, for despite his addiction to the Three R's, Schoolin was only too happy to forsake the paths of syllabus for the world around.

The rainbow was one of his recurring favourites, for in the

frequent interludes of storm and sunshine, the marriage of sun and rain often produced huge arches of phenomenal brightness in the washed country air that could span the sky from the Garn Fawr tumulus to the Abermawr sea.

'Fold arms and sit up.' After the familiar command, Schoolin designated the arc through the school window, using his cane to conduct a symphony of colours.

'Orange, yellow, green, blue. Now where did those colours come from? Anybody?'

A hand shot aloft before his son, with half-understood, show-off explanations bubbling from his *Children's Encyclopaedias*, could answer.

'Please sir, God paints it to show it's stopped raining. Like Noah in the ark.' Willie Jones was the son of a local lay preacher. His thinking already had a theological tinge as he was hoping to become a minister, and was about to join the County School Scholarship candidates at the back of the class.

'Well, yes, Willie, you could put it like that. But how does He do it?'

Willie came back like a flash, 'Please sir, no man can know God . . .'

'Right, I'll tell you,' said Schoolin, deciding to ignore the challenge from the young Baptist and he lifted a paperweight prism from his desk into the path of a sunbeam. But his explanation had hardly begun before the open door admitted an intruder which radically ousted the spectrum from Schoolin's mind.

Greta Perkins, a ten-year-old sitting in the front row, shot up her hand with a gasp. 'Please sir, a snake!'

Waddling somewhat, under her load, came Butterpaws,

Llewelyn's cat. The snake, displaying the clearly-marked Vs of an adder, was gripped behind the head so that eighteen inches of wriggling body were being lugged along the ground. Suddenly, with the strength of a leopard, Butterpaws leapt on to Schoolin's desk, to show off her prey. The cat, however, landed on the schoolmaster's blotter, which flew across the polished surface, taking its unusual cargo with it and, in the process of falling off the other side, Butterpaws lost her hold on the snake. Being freshly caught and still very much alive, the snake began to wriggle towards the first desk, where Greta Perkins and her sister Dolly stood up on their seats and now began to scream in earnest.

'Goddlemighty,' cried Schoolin, forgetting himself for a moment, and rushing round, crushed the adder's head with his size twelve boot (under which many an old rat made slow by age had also met its end, running across the back yard to the sty, to steal the pig's food).

With half the senior school now standing on the desks and Miss Prothero peering in goggle-eyed alarm round the door of the infant's room, Schoolin calmed the uproar with a bellowed, 'Quiet there', and with his foot still on the adder sent his son to fetch the garden fork. This was used to carry the snake to the midden where it rested until sundown, to ensure that its mate was not around. Jimmy James, that expert on furred animals, later told Llewelyn that you should 'never have a kitten born in May, because they always brings home snakes', which was surely a case of being wise after the event because Jimmy had himself given Llewelyn Butterpaws, a May-time kitten, only the year before.

The lore of St Nicholas children contained numerous beliefs of this kind. The presence of the yellow hammer indicated an adder was near and yellow of any kind was a sinister colour to beware and avoid in animals and birds. Adders chased human beings, by revolving like hoops. Weasels must never be attacked because they had a special scream too high to hear, which called the tribe to their aid; and weasels and stoats attacked by leaping at the throat, so a woollen scarf should always be worn for protection. Bats were poisonous, should never be touched. Owls went straight for your eyes. Otters had jaws strong enough to crack your knee, the badger

was unkillable. There was a deep fear of being bitten by a mad dog or a mad fox, because you became mad yourself and went round biting other people. A bird flying against a bedroom window meant death. When lightning was going to strike a house there was always a smell of sulphur. Imitating someone's facial expression was very dangerous, because if the wind changed, your face would retain the shape for life. Even Llewelyn's grandmother sometimes made use of that when her grandson was 'pulling faces'.

There were other less dramatic interruptions of the timetable than the adder. Members of the Management Committee called, not just to snap-check and sign the Registers as being accurate, but to ride their own special hobby horses as well. 'Mrs Harris, Tregwynt, visited school and gave two prizes for the best essays on Patriotism written by the 1st class children – Beryl Jones and Bessie Luke won the 1st and 2nd prizes respectively of 2s. 6d. and 1s. 6d.'

'Mrs John, Trellys, called at the school and offered a 1s. prize for the best writing out of H.M. King George's Six Maxims.'

There were others who arrived in the classic mode, bearing gifts, like for example, Mr C. A. Roberts, the retired manager of Lloyds Bank, Fishguard – bank clerks were revered in the parish as shining examples of 'getting on' – who called at the school for which he had, as a small boy, helped to collect donations to get the school built, and which he had subsequently attended as one of the first pupils. A few days after his visit he sent a registered envelope to the school with a silver florin for every pupil. The headmaster's Log Book for that day records that the pupils 'instructed the Headmaster to write to Mr. Roberts conveying to him thanks and Best Love for his kindness'.

But even without the intervention of rainbows, snakes and bank managers, the St Nicholas school day was seldom allowed to drag for Schoolin leavened the labours of the Three R's with plenty of

25

variety, both for his own sake as well as the children's. There was an interlude of singing every day, always a poem (the children's favourites were The Fairies, The Brook, The Tiger, The Daffodils, Horatius, John Gilpin, Lochinvar, but most often the school was to be heard chanting 'Up the airy mountain, down the rushy glen'.) There would also be a story reading – favourites were Gerard's *Long Journey* (abridged from *The Cloister and the Hearth*) *Tales from the Mabinogion, Coral Island, Treasure Island, Scenes from Dickens, Robinson Crusoe*– and there were improvised sessions involving reminiscences of The Rebecca Riots – the burning of Welsh toll gates by Welshmen dressed as women.

Especially there were highly-coloured stories about the fiery Welsh doctor William Price of Llantrisant, the first to practice cremation, who, on a morning in September 1870, dressed in his customary finery – white tunic, scarlet-braided, brass-buttoned waistcoat, green pixie trousers, long hair in plaits and on his head, the fox skin from which the head and legs still dangled – had driven his horse and gig at speed into Schoolin's grandfather's farmyard, had selected and bought a Welsh Black calf of the right size, cut its throat in the byre, sawn off a piece of the thigh bone and then rushed it away for grafting to the leg of a young collier injured in a pit-roof fall.

History came gleefully to life with tales of Alfred burning the cakes, the exploits of Hereward the Wake, Owen Glyndwr, Llewelyn the Great and other Welsh heroes, the lore of druids. Geography was dominated by the highest mountains, longest rivers, deepest oceans, tallest trees, the mystery of why the seas did not fall off the round earth, stories of anacondas and octopus and whales, the sagas of Francis Drake and Scott of the Antarctic, Pygmies and Hottentots, of coal and gold. Morality and prudence were taught through the medium of Aesop's *Fables*, a great Schoolin favourite.

There were also a number of set-pieces, especially savoured because they gave play to the schoolmaster's love of the heroic and epic, and were well suited to his semi-operatic style of teaching. On Empire Day special lessons dealing with the British Empire and its influence 'on civilisation were given by the Headmaster, suitable songs and hymns were sung and the proceedings closed with the singing of "God Save the King".' Later, 'A lesson on Armistice Observation, Peace Among the Nations, and the League of Nations, was given to the whole school by the Headmaster, suitable hymns were then sung, and the *Nunc Dimitis* was sung before dismissal . . .' (The Log always reported Royal occasions with a special flourish of rhetoric. 'Royal Wedding of the Duke of Gloucester and the Lady Alice and the school closed for the day *by Royal Command.*' The school closed for the Duke of York's wedding '*by the Command of the King*'.)

Syllabus-bending Schoolin, with his thigh-slapping enthusiasms for oddities, eccentrics and apochrypha of all kinds, was never a favourite with the reigning Director of Education. But the success of the school both in the Three R's and in the County School Scholarships ensured that he received plenty of support from parents and Managers. A typical School Managers' Minute reads, '. . . cordially congratulated the Headmaster for the excellent results obtained by his pupils in the Scholarship examination for the secondary schools . . . and the Members of the Board desired to emphasize that there were five successes to record which is really creditable for a small country school.'

Before such events were routine, he held 'Open Days' to put the work of his pupils on display. On 26 October 1925 the Log entry reads, 'School open to parents and friends today. . . . A children's Exhibition was opened by the Rector when about 200 articles representing Art, Carton Work, Needlework, Raffia work and Basketry were on view. . . . The Exhibition was re-opened at 7 p.m., when there was a crowded attendance . . .'

Those St Nicholas pupils who contributed articles to School Exhibitions in the late 1920s remember particularly the name of Cyril James, brother of Jimmy the little Mole King. A slight, quiet boy with a heart-shaped face, he could draw with the fidelity of a camera. He enshrined cathedrals and cottages, cats and dogs, flowers and nanny goats, liners and lambs, swinging bells and sleeping tigers, in pencilled drawings exquisitely rendered with light and shade. A section of school wall on the Open Day was a sort of private exhibition by Cyril. Schoolin endeavoured several times to convince his parents that Cyril should be apprenticed as a draughtsman and perhaps even become an architect but the obstacle of 5s. a week indenture money stood in the way. So Cyril left school at fourteen, and like most of his comrades went to work on a farm for the pittance wage of the day. The long sensitive hands which could weave shapes and vistas of light and shade with those magic pencils – which he kept proudly in a special pencil box in which the top swivelled to reveal a second compartment of coloured chalks – soon calloused and coarsened, the promise of bright fulfilment shrivelled and two years after leaving school, he fell off a hay wain, broke his back and died.

CHAPTER TWO

The Call of the Meadow

'. . . *a lecture on temperance was given to the Scholars this morning.*'
Headmaster's Log Book, 14 May 1925

'. . . *Ivor Evans (absent) helping with the sheep . . .*'
Headmaster's Log Book, 26 April 1926

The schoolmaster began his morning in the chill gloaming of the flagstoned back kitchen of School House where he washed with carbolic soap in cold well water, stropped his cut-throat razor on oiled leather, lathered his beard with more carbolic, rasped the stubble noisily off his face and trimmed his moustache. He knuckle-gouged his eyes with a faintly squelching sound before donning gold-rimmed pince-nez.

Buttoning the sleeves of his Welsh flannel shirt, he walked the few paces into the kitchen where black boots cleaned by Nana his sister-in-law shone in the fender, and Boof the one-eyed black tom – who, after disappearing and surviving three years of feral rabbit-gorging, had returned home in his old age – stared, unwinking as a yogi, at the flames.

'Boof, Boof,' he said in mildly admonishing tones, 'you're an old idlepack and no mistake. Starting to rest as soon as you get up.'

He reached on the mantelpiece for his collar and tie – for no discernible reason, collars and ties were always taken off and left downstairs in the Welsh villages of those days – and tied a loose large knot which barely concealed the stud. He always had a faintly dishevelled, countryman appearance (even in his Sunday best) and, apart from shaving, never sought his image in a mirror, from one year's end to another.

Now the thought of breakfast filled his world and he cut and pressed three thick slices of home-baked brown bread horizontally and vertically against the glowing firebars to score them with carbonised crosses, topped up the sullen heap of grounds in the pot and poured out a reeking waterfall of black coffee. A Carmarthenshire farmer's son, diverted into teaching to thin out the ratio of sons to available acres, he still ate and drank with smacking gusto in a countryman's table stoop – which has its point, for crouching address to the table cuts the distance from plate to mouth and saves time when work is calling. Rolling a cigarette from his cylindrical paper packet of Shag with its thin red tracing, he rose, smelling of carbolic soap, tobacco, earth and Welsh tweed from the local cloth mill.

The schoolmaster was now ready for the outside world, and calling a cheerful goodbye to his wife Catherine who had breakfast in bed, he squashed on an ancient trilby, climbed the stone steps and made for his garden.

Pulling back the bolt, he stood a moment, luxuriating in his vegetable Goshen, noticed little mole-heaved hillocks in his carrot bed and made a mental note to set a trap. He walked among the cabbages and chose a football-hearted monster for the day's dinner, pausing at the pig sty on his return to strip and throw in the outer leaves and the earth-covered root. As the tribute landed in the trough, the grunting tenant emerged and Schoolin gazed with satisfaction at the waddling colossus, savouring for a moment the sensual odour of pig body rising from the sty. He dropped a few cinders off the wall pile, which the sow began to crunch noisily like walnuts.

'Blodwen love,' Schoolin said with a lift of his arm like a butcher's blessing, 'you're going to be an old beauty and no mistake. Carry on, girl.'

He walked briskly up the village street, past the shop to Spring Gardens Farm where the morning quart of milk, still not quite cool from the cow's hot udder, waited in the dairy where the air smelled as though it had been blown through butter milk. He called at the smithy, the clearing house of parish gossip, for a few minutes, to keep abreast of the recent doings and misdoings in the parish and returned home ready to start the day's work.

The visitor about to arrive at the school that morning had been laid on by the Squire, who was a non-conformist autocrat for whom alcoholic drink of all kinds, even the homebrew of harvest, was sinful and who resolutely refused to put the souls, bodies (or rents) of his tenants, at risk – he owned most of the houses in the village – through the temptations of a village pub. The Squire was also Chairman of the Managers, and as the children settled into their desks after the Register, Collars Morgan, the day's monitor (and boss of the school peck order) – who was in his last year and spent much of his time staring out of the window at the countryside where he would soon be earning his living as a fourteen-year-old farm worker, for eighty percent of the boys who left school went to work on farms – shot his hand into the air like a rocket, determined to be first with the news.

'Please sir, a man on a bicycle coming to school . . .'

The visitor was pushing his bike laboriously up the incline and when he arrived, the children, cued by Schoolin's cane, rose and chanted, 'Good morning, sir,' a communal greeting which the new arrival acknowledged with an old-fashioned bow.

'Fold arms,' Schoolin ordered. Experience showed that a crossed arm posture exercised a tranquillising effect during waiting periods.

Mr Owen was a bachelor, living on his own, who did a bit of many things for a livelihood. He mended boots, painted and papered, and operated as a part-time herbalist, with a faded front room sign which read 'Natural Cures for Natural Illness'. As befitted one of his principles he was a great believer in keeping the system thoroughly irrigated with well water. A deacon in the local chapel and a pillar of the Band of Hope, his hatred of drink stemmed from his early life in which a drunken father had kept the family poverty-stricken and who had met his death when walking home drunk one Saturday night, by falling into a ditch and drowning in a few inches of water.

Mr Owen was tall and bamboo-thin, and his turtle neck was encased in a celluloid collar, round the inside rim of which he now ran a forefinger with a grimace of relief. His rolling black eyes and drooping moustache gave him something of the appearance of an old-fashioned villain in a Victorian melodrama and it was sometimes a little difficult to take him quite seriously.

While the infants were being joined on to the Big School, he placed his brown suitcase flat on Schoolin's desk, and began to chat with the schoolmaster. He spoke in superlatives.

'Ah, Mr Jones,' he said, pressing in closely, so that Schoolin made half a step backwards, 'I am very, very pleased to meet you. I am indeed very, very glad today was so convenient for you. I propose to take up at very most half an hour of the school's time.' He looked vaguely at the blackboard where the eleven times table was hanging in prominence. 'I know it may have to come off sums, but it will be time very, very well spent if we wean only one little soul from future sin. For as you well know, Mr Jones, there is more joy in heaven over one sinner repented than over one or two million righteous.'

He seemed inspired by the sunlight falling through the squire's trees.

'Wonderful spring we are having, following a wonderful winter and now it looks as though a wonderful summer is ahead. We have a wonderful wonderful lot to be thankful for, isn't it?'

'Indeed, indeed,' Schoolin agreed quickly, and seeing that Mr Owen appeared to be ready, introduced him to the waiting children.

'Now, boys and girls, here is Mr Owen who has cycled all the way from Letterston to talk to us about something important, so I want you to listen very carefully to what he has to say.' He concluded with a warning lift of his cane, 'And I don't want any noise now, mind. So pay attention.'

Mr Owen walked two steps forward and one to the right which put him in front of Schoolin's desk, and began his address.

'Well, boys and girls, the headmaster Mr Jones has introduced me as Mr Owen, Letterston. Plain Mr Owen as you might say. But there is more to me than that. Oh dear me yes, boys and girls. You see my full name is Mr Owen Philadelphia Owen, and I was baptised like that because my grandfather really did go to Philadelphia in the morning, like the man in the song!'

The school remained solemn, vaguely suspecting geography, but when Mr Owen bared tombstone teeth with a 'Ha, Ha, He, He', and Schoolin gave an accompanying guffaw, the children began to follow suit, though they never understood the joke. It was a moment of only passing levity anyhow for Mr Owen now began his task in earnest.

'I have come by here', he said, in doomster tones, 'to warn you about drinking. Boys and girls, you are young and your lives are before you. But you are not too young to have heard of the Drink. For Drink is. the work of the Deevil' – Mr Owen spoke key words in capital letters and his Deevil rhymed with Evil – 'and indeed you could say that Drink is just another word for the *Deevil* himself.'

For upwards of fifteen minutes, he developed his theme with conviction and relish – sometimes brushing his moustache with a rapid sideways motion as though to sharpen the ends – connecting Drink with the Fall, and speaking frequently of the Deevil being 'pushed down from Heaven on his 'ead'. Then leaning forward, he pointed at the class and shouted, '. . . and the Drink could bring you – and you – and you . . .' impaling the open-mouthed audience one by one with his forefinger, including the smallest children for whom 'drink' meant only water or cocoa – '*down down down* . . .' and as he repeated the words he bent his legs in a sort of wishbone bend as though to draw a gun. He fingered his moustache, walked for a moment up and down in front of the school, giving the children a moment to ponder his warnings, and then gave a trumpeting two-handed noseblow as though announcing that the most important part of his performance was about to begin.

He now took from the suitcase on Schoolin's desk a bottle labelled 'Whisky', poured a little into the white enamel saucer which he carried, held it up, before the class for a moment and then carried it to Schoolin's desk. He took a box of matches from his pocket, extracted a match, and pointing to the saucer said, – 'Boys and girls, that is W.H.I.S.K.Y,' and he spelled out the letters in a spine-chilling stage whisper, 'and it will burn you up like F.I.R.E,' and as he again spelled out the word he held a lighted match to the saucer which began to burn with a blue flame. Mr Owen held it forward to show the class, at the same time lifting his left hand as though to keep off any draughts. The flame died, the saucer was returned to the desk and now he took out from his case three jars.

They were chillingly labelled 'Heart of a Drunkard', 'What Alcohol does to your Liver', and one, misspelled, 'Kidley of a

Whisky Fiend'. The children passed them round as though they might bite or blow up, though the following day in the playground, John Price, son of a drunken Trefasser butcher, said his father had told him, after a description of the bottles, that they were only the innards of a nanny goat. But before Butcher Price's devaluation, the feeling was one of goggle-eyed awe.

Mr Owen again impaled the school with a pointing forefinger and said, 'Now that you boys and girls know what the Drink will do to your body and soul, hands up all those who will sign the Pledge and save themselves when they are old enough,' but the class seemed mesmerised and not a hand was raised until Schoolin gave his stentorian instruction.

'Hands up everybody at once,' and, big and small alike, the hands of the entire school shot up and remained aloft in witness until the bellow 'Hands down' was heard.

This was the only time in the course of Mr Owen's visits that response had to be commanded for when the forest of hands had fallen, Mr Owen arrived at Rewards, and taking out a large bag of Band-of-Hope peardrops from his suitcase his whole personality seemed to soften, his face became gleeful and tender and he began to dole out the goodies into palms, with the words, 'There now, that's good, isn't it, that's for being good children.' Knowledge that witness earned *peardrops*, always afterwards brought instant promise of future abstinence.

His role of sugar daddy over, Mr Owen left his sucking converts with a last cunning exhortation.

'Be faithful to the Band of Hope, Sign the Pledge, and stick to Adam's Ale and you will be halfway to heaven, a lovely Beulah-land of harps and peardrops and crystal clear water.'

On Schoolin's command, he was clapped and when he had packed his treasures, the school rose to chant, 'Good morning,

B

Mr Owen Sir.' They watched him push his bicycle down the road to the kitchen of the Squire.

Schoolin watched for a moment with a smile, and then to compensate for what the children might see as a lapse, frowned mightily, restoring decorum with shouts about the next lesson, bringing his cane down on the desk blotting pad with a thwack. But Mr Owen's visit appeared to have given the pupils a special burst of energy, for there was exceptional resonance in the spelling chorus which followed his visit to the Big Room and the injunction to 'change 'y' into 'i' and add 'es' for plurals of words ending in 'y', hit the rafters like a boomerang.

What effect Mr Owen's warnings had on the future drinking habits of the pupils would be impossible to assess. In any case, anybody reading the Headmaster's Log for that time might be excused for giving the squire's concern with the future temperance of the school a relatively low priority compared, say, to the present temperature of the schoolroom. There are some chilling references in the Log '. . . a frosty morning with temperature down to 38 degrees. The heating arrangement is inadequate for the room and so temperature only reached 44 degrees at midday. Several children absent with colds.' The entry for the following day reads, 'Much coughing among those present . . .' After sustained agitation and protest, Schoolin eventually obtained the new Tortoise stove – in time for Midsummer's Day.

It could be argued, even more strongly, that future drinking habits had an even lower priority compared with the present eating habits of some children. Many of the dinners were eloquent commentary on a countryside with more stones than soil and where the grip of agricultural depression was grim. Farms teetered on the verge of bankruptcy, farm workers were paid 28s. for a fifty-four-

hour, six-day week, farmers received 10d. a lb for their butter, 6d. a dozen for eggs.

The need for unpaid labour on the farm had a continuing effect on Attendance, constantly reflected in the Log: 'Several families are absent picking potatoes with their parents', 'the bigger boys were absent today, driving cattle and pigs to Letterston Monthly Fair', 'bigger boys are assisting parents with the grain', 'five children absent attending to the threshing . . .'

The constant dinner staple of farm workers' children was home-made buns which became as hard as the well capstone by the next baking – you could usually count the currants of two buns on the fingers of one hand – and potatoes ready baked in their jackets for re-heating on the backs of the tortoises. Farmers' children did better, bringing fat bacon and bread. Farm children also brought milk in small medicine bottles, and watery cocoa with condensed milk was served to the stove-huddling children in winter. Schoolin made many attempts to obtain fresh milk for the poorer children but, as the Minutes of the Managers' meeting of 20 March 1937 record, 'could not secure a vendor who was willing to comply with the health regulations of the milk control', because of the often insanitary conditions on the farms. So he insisted on Cod Liver Oil and Malt for the especially needy children through the winter and also obtained boots for some from parish relief.

Schoolin pushed open the dragging frame and zinc door that led from his backyard to the school. The pastoral music of Parc Davis came to his ears. The meadow was hardly more than a long angler's cast from the school and each May the apprentice bleats of lambs and the gruff answers of the mother ewes joined the song of the Three R's through the open school windows.

William Davis, the meadow owner from whom Schoolin purchased his morning milk, was a school manager, sometimes a little morose and introspective when gripped by sad memories of the event which had left him a childless widower. But mostly he was mild and kind and prepared to take pains to co-operate with the school and, each year, the farmer's son turned school-master (always avid to reinvest in his farming childhood), set his older pupils the task of writing a composition on the lambing scene nearby. As the birdsong and bleating pulled him away from the school door that afternoon, Schoolin, as he often did, made a snap teaching decision and, for the second time that day, walked briskly to Spring Gardens.

Concealing shrewd scrutiny of the widower's mood behind a smile, he answered the expression of interrogative surprise at this second visit.

'In view of the fact it's such a fine day, I wondered whether you could spare a quarter of an hour today for your talk to the Big School about the lambs. That is, if it's convenient, of course.'

Dudgeon and melancholy were far away from the widower on this Maytime afternoon as the Big Room pupils gathered around him at the entrance to his meadow.

Burly, slightly stooping, the heavily-moustached, trilby-hatted figure – continuously shirt-sleeved from spring to autumn – wasted no time in beginning. Embracing the flock with a wide sweep of his arm, he said, 'When you visit the sheep at lambing time, always look first for the ewe on her own, away from the flock.'

He pointed to a white-faced ewe, alone in a corner of the meadow.

'There,' he said, in his lilting Welsh voice, 'see, look at her, she's scraping the earth with her foot, trying to make a sort of nest for her lamb, like the wild sheep used to do, long ago. Now watch her, watch her. She's lying down and look, see how her head is pointing to the sky. It's a sure sign she's going to begin lambing,' and indeed, within minutes, the first lamb of twins was leaving the womb.

Each year, the happenings in Parc Davis dramatised the gamut of life and death for the village school. In autumn – with accompanying ribald comment from the older ones – the children surreptitiously watched the rams at work among the ewes. In spring they watched the ewes giving birth and – as is inevitable in any flock – saw some lambs and ewes die as well.

William Davis set out to defeat the consequences of death in the flock by ensuring that, as far as was humanly possible, all the surviving lambs were reared naturally on mother's milk, and none was brought up artificially as a 'pet lamb' on the bottle. It demanded great shepherding skill and dedication.

The farmer paused in his disquisition and the lilting voice remained silent for a short time as he watched the progress of the nearby birth. One lamb was already born and the head of the second had appeared. In the short silence of his scrutiny, a curious lamb approached within a few yards of the gate. The mother followed, with bleating solicitude, nosing and smelling her offspring. Careful not to make any sudden movement to startle them away, the farmer pointed to the lamb, and then sought out

Collars Morgan with the question, 'What's special about that lamb then, Peter Morgan?'

Without a moment's hesitation, Collars, who would soon himself be involved with such problems, replied, 'It's got two skins.'

'Quite right, quite right. The ewe's own lamb died and I put the dead lamb's skin on this lamb, so it would smell the same and get adopted.'

For a few more minutes he developed the theme of lamb recognition by smell among the ewes and then the pastoral interlude was ended and the children returned reluctantly to class to begin the composition on 'How to be a good shepherd', based on the tricks and stratagems of William Davis's shepherding craft. During the days following, drawings and cut-outs appeared in profusion, pasted on the distempered walls of the Big Room, and even the Little Room had its own plasticine weirdies, standing or leaning or falling over on the desks of Miss Prothero's modelling toddlers. For a week each spring, therefore, the school was alive with the pastoral drama of the Parc Davis meadow.

Always in fine-weather dinner times, there was a group of children round the little pond formed by the outflow from the village well – which was only fifty yards from the school – stoning coots, chasing ducks, searching for minnows and sticklebacks or lying flat on the flagstones to advance head first into the cold gloaming under the granite cap where springs bubbled through the gravel, tiny whirly-gig beetles revolved like water-tops, rod-shaped insects skated with gossamer feet, and water boatmen rowed upside down, the stuntmen of the well.

This particular dinner hour, Tusks Evans was standing on the capstone, feet close together, proudly showing off the pair of new black boots which his mother had bought him in Fishguard.

Appropriately, it was eleven-year-old Clogs Evans – who had the complexion and craftiness of a young reynard and was so called for his noisy clod-hoppering footwear – who set about cutting Tusks and his new boots down to size.

With what was meant to be a large wink to the world at large, somewhat spoiled by both eyes being closed at the same time, he

said, 'I'll tell yer wot, Tusks, I'll tell yer wot. I bet yer boots won't stop the water by there . . .' and he pointed with treacherous surmise to the fast outflow of the pipe. 'I'll tell yer wot,' he added, 'I'll bet yer three sloes,' and he made a motion of feeling the wager in his corduroy pocket.

By far the youngest of the group which cohered loosely into the village gang, Tusks felt constrained to treat every challenge as an assertion of his great age and worthiness and although the outflow was nine inches deep he jumped off the capstone and dangled a valiant toe in the outflow.

'Go on, mun Tusks,' added Gwynfor Bowen, another eleven-year-old (nicknamed Voices because his rabbit trapper father was a male voice choir leader), 'Wot's the matter, you frightened or suffin?'

It may be that Tusks would have rebutted this charge of cowardice anyhow but the devil suddenly entered Voices and he gave Tusks a push so that he overbalanced with both feet into the outflow which rose above his ankles and filled his boots. Just at that moment, Schoolin appeared, vigorously agitating the handbell

to call the brood to the sung Grace that began the afternoon session.

'Ha, ha, ha,' shouted Clogs, signing the air with two empty palms, 'aint got no sloes, aint got no sloes,' and a tearful Tusks squelched after his elders, to sit with wet feet through the afternoon, in the course of which another visitor was about to arrive at the school with more trouble in store for his bodily comfort.

Nurse Price arrived that day, as always, driving in a Governess Car. She was a short, stout, rather intimidating lady, with a round red face and pebble-lensed glasses. With Schoolin's permission, she ran her hand along the school surfaces to monitor the cleaner's work, spoke to the children about the dangers of dirt and ringworm (ringworm was dreaded because the children believed that if the ring or rings met, it meant death), and dirty teeth. She also examined the older girls for signs of incipient goitre, a condition much feared, and not infrequently found in the parish of those days.

She also poked her nose briefly into the 'offices', known as the 'stinkers', the spaces fronting which were respectively No-Boys'- or Girls'-Land, though there were occasions when the schoolmaster's legs were safely under the dinner table and Miss Prothero absent for some reason when the older girls, linked arm in arm, lined up on the edge of the boys' territory to provoke a grinning barrage, with plenty of ribald mime from the older bucks which sometimes led to flushed faces and screams and even wrestling on the grass. Sometimes the boys came slinking round the girls' corner to bawl remarks into the occupied offices.

'Hurry up there, Nancy, I'm comin' in in a minnit . . .'

'Coo, wot a stink, must be Bronwen Pugh . . .' and similar threats and insults which produced shrieks and threats to tell Schoolin.

But, above all, Miss Price was concerned with heads and hair and, as usual, on this afternoon, the school waited with folded arms for Schoolin's stentorian command – 'Heads Down' – the mandatory posture of the search for nits. The older children all passed the test that day, but when Nurse Price arrived at Tusks, her probing fingers and X-ray eyes quickly showed his basin crop to be tenanted and the wet-foot little culprit was then marched into the porch, his head bowed over a large sheet of blotting paper and painfully scoured with a 'toothcomb', the teeth so fine and close together that the most cunning nit or hidden egg was hardly likely to escape.

There was no disgrace in the eyes of the children in having the presence of nits established – it even conferred a certain status on the host – though when Tusks returned home, with a note and a toothcomb, his hard-pressed mother took a different view. She blamed his condition on Illtyd Morris, the gypsy boy who lived in a caravan near the sea, a notorious carrier of livestock in his dishevelled poll. Illtyd was absent from school that day, and indeed made only sporadic appearances, and was the despair of the 'whipper-in', the Attendance Officer who travelled on a sputtering motorcycle named – so it was believed – 'James', armoured all season in goggles, leather helmet and thick fawn waterproofs, like a man from Mars.

The nurse came once a month. The school dentist called twice a year and is remembered by Llewelyn not for his skills, which were of a root and branch character based on extraction, but because he provided first intimation that being Schoolin's son meant nothing where the System was concerned. The young Llewelyn sat with folded arms with the rest of the infants, waiting in the Little Room under Miss Prothero's eye. The door was opened and a man in a white coat appeared, carrying horizontally with both hands a case of gleamingly polished wood. As he opened the case, and set out a glass jar, into which he poured a pink liquid, he waved a gleaming instrument and said like a liveried child butcher, 'Right, I'll have the first one . . .'

Schoolin's son watched in terror, as victim after victim was delivered to the White Fiend, placed on the torture stool, and reduced to tears. But not till the end did he believe that he would be passed to the Mouth Mohock by his own father and when Schoolin uttered the unbelievable words, 'Next child there', clung

to his desk like a limpet until Schoolin came over with a stranger's grin to winkle him off, and put to the sword and with the terrible steel filling his mouth, he was reduced to gurgling screams.

Schoolin too had (short-lived) difficulties with the System, for in the early part of his St Nicholas headship he experienced an almost comic degree of interference from his Managers. The Squire and Mrs Davies, the elderly aristocratic widow from the neighbouring parish manor, together with the elderly vicar in charge when Schoolin first arrived, made intolerant by illness and a bored, superior wife, had been accustomed to exercise a degree of interference in day to day school detail, unimaginable today. A minuted injunction 'expressed the opinion that the head teacher should himself supervise the children during their dinner', that 'the Managers agreed the morning playtime at 11 o'clock should be limited to 5 minutes . . . it was felt country children had sufficient exercise in walking to and from school.' At the same meeting, the Managers minuted the solemn decision 'that the ventilator in the school be closed during the winter months'. They had also been accustomed, without schoolmaster participation, to decide the date and duration of school holidays. But these displays of authoritarianism did not last long after Schoolin's arrival anyhow for, apart from the fact that he would not have tolerated it, when the elderly cleric was translated, he was replaced by the Reverend Isaiah Jenkins and the schoolmaster was able to exercise fully his rights and writ, with the blessing of the boisterous ordinand from Cardiganshire.

CHAPTER THREE

The Schoolmaster at Home

*'The Chairman read a letter received that morning from
Mr J. Ll. Jones, withdrawing his application for the post of
Head Teacher . . . because he considered the house available
in the village too small.'*

School Managers' Minutes, 12 July 1922

Schoolin's house was one of seventeen in a village shaped rather
like a capital 'T'. Along the top stroke were the Squire's stone-built
residence with its large garden and orchard, the two tiny
cottages where a farm worker and the old school cleaner lived, the
house of the tailor, shopkeeper, carpenter, a tiny smallholding, the
large rectory, and a rabbit trapper's smallholding. On the other side
of the road was the smithy, another smallholding and Spring
Gardens Farm. Along the down stroke lived a roadman, a middle-
aged dying consumptive, another rabbit trapper, the schoolmaster
and his smallholder neighbour. Overlooking the village, on the
granite eminence of Garn Llys – a part, as it were, of the changeless
furniture of the village landscape – was the burial monument or
cromlech, Samson's Quoit, a perennial playing ground of
generations of village children.

On this particular evening just before sunset, Llewelyn and
his friends rode on bucking chargers round the tomb on which the
latest victim of the stone knife lay prone, invisible except for the
soles of his boots.

He was clearly not quite dead for he suddenly sat upright, to
reveal a moony sort of face, faintly anxious too, as though he
feared being forgotten. The face was topped by a basin crop of
uncombed black hair.

This evidence of life outraged the leader who pulled his horse
of forked sycamore to a kicking, neighing halt and shrilled, 'Get
down by there, Tusks, mun. You fool, you aint got no heart, you'm
bloomin dead . . .' and as the heartless victim fell back obediently,
the charge recommenced to cries of 'Tusks is dead, dead, dead . . .'

The leader stopped, and the red-sky silence round the cromlech
was complete. He grew aware of the disappearing sun, the shadows
of hawthorns shaped by scissoring winds, groups of rooks winging
to the rookery elms. He suddenly wanted to go home.

The cromlech victim sat upright again and, unchided this time,
swung his legs over the side and began to slither to the ground.
The figures erupted into life, horses momentarily ran out of
control, demanding discipline from riding crops of bracken. The
leader began to bawl in a cracking voice the words of the song
which were sweeping the parish.

'Show me the way to go 'ome, H'm tired and H'i wants to go
to bed . . .' and looking round as though to collect his troupe he
shouted, 'Good legs it is, you duffers' – a word borrowed from
Schoolin – and set off with a gailop down the gorse and heather
slope towards the village.

'I 'ad a little drink about a hower ago and it's gone right to my
'ead . . .' the song continued, and the Welsh accent clung to the
words as thick as molasses.

'Wait for me, wait for me . . .' The little boy's tones were tearful
now and Llewelyn stopped, looked round, and waited for his

companion, moved by his gnomic smallness, his difficulty in getting through the gorse.

'Cor, Tusks, you done well on the Quoit. You looked really dead,' said Llewelyn to encourage him. He took his hand and together they went stumbling over the ant heaps which littered the gorse-strewn heath.

At the crossroads they found Clogs and Gwynfor, the latter lying stunned in the road where he had been thrown by his horse shying violently at a barn owl, swooping on silent wings through the gloaming.

'Blooming goodyhoo done it,' said Clogs, gazing with satisfaction at Gwynfor and touching the prone figure with his boot. Suddenly he threw back his head and, baring his teeth, began to screech a succession of long drawn-out 'goodyhoos'. Llewelyn and Tusks joined in and the white Shorthorns from Spring Gardens Farm lifted their heads, stared for a moment in the direction of the noise and then resumed grazing. As though the owl cries had restored him to life, Gwynfor stood up and joined the hooters. Slashing with his sycamore wand at the bats jinking through the air like fly-halves, sometimes so close as to make the boys duck their heads, Gwyn led his companions full pelt to the village where light from the first cottage wavered across the road. Clogs raised his hand, 'Abyssinia,' he said and lifted the latch on the faded front door.

'Abyssinia,' echoed the three. Gwynfor sped past the shop towards his home, while Llewelyn and Tusks turned left along the down stroke of the village and as they parted in the darkness Llewelyn hopped on one leg down three stone steps, and lifted the noisy latch.

The light poured out for a moment as he passed into the kitchen.

It was a long narrow room dominated at one end by the fireplace spanning wall to wall, and the special cosiness of which had finally decided Schoolin's wife, Catherine, to make the move to St Nicholas from their big house at the Cardiganshire village of St Dogmaels. In the corner by the fireside oven, his grandmother, Ba, was sitting, dressed in black. The cat Butterpaws (so christened because Jimmy the Mole Catcher who had given her to Llewelyn had told Llewelyn to rub her paws with butter to stop her returning to her mother) was asleep on her voluminously skirted lap.

Next to her sat Schoolin, deep into a book with a familiar binding, for with the arrival of the darker evenings, he eased himself into what became each winter an orgy of Dickens, though his evenings were often subject to interruptions while he filled in forms for the farmers, prepared accounts, discussed wills, wrote letters, advised worried parents, clerked for the Parish Council. Each year he read as many novels as he could get through, beginning always with *Pickwick Papers* and aiming to end with *Edwin Drood*. As reading progressed, the favourite Dickens scenes became part of life in the kitchen, and as winter advanced he became more and more possessed by the Dickens eccentrics and mention of the names alone were a touch-paper to set mirth roaring through the winter's night: 'Tupman', and then again 'Tupman' (over and over again), 'Snubbins', 'Snodgrass', 'Fogg', 'Mr Veller', and each stoked the laughter until it roared like the kitchen chimney as Schoolin bared his teeth and slapped the oak arm of his armchair, and took off his pince-nez to wipe his streaming eyes. Tonight, he had not quite got into his winter stride, and was content to chuckle aloud at Mr Jingle's doings.

Llewelyn's mother was reading a novel by Allen Raine, and Nana, her sister, seated at the end nearest the door, was immersed in the

latest *Family Herald* episode of 'The Moonstone', soundlessly
moving her lips as she read. The tall table lamp, with its polished
brass reservoir, clear glass globe and twin wicks of flame, painted
the walls with gold, except at the far end of the table where Nana's
candle boosted the waning lamplight.

Schoolin raised his hand in absent-minded greeting to his son.
His mother looked up, and her eyes shone.

'Ah Llewelyn, there you are, then. I wondered where you were.'

She looked at the spotty-faced alarm clock ticking on the
mantelpiece and then at the dark curtainless window.

'Where've you been tonight then?'

'Samson's Quoit,' Llewelyn replied. 'We've been sacrificing
Tusks Evans. We cut out his heart with a stone knife and we all
ate it while he was alive.'

'Gracious me, what terrible things children say today. I don't
know where they get it all from . . .' said his mother.

Llewelyn slipped like an eel between table and wall, sat on the
stool in front of the place laid for his supper. His mother opened
the fireside oven door and the air was charged with delicious
smells. Holding the enamel plate with a heat-resisting hessian pad,
his mother paused for a moment and with a sidelong glance and
a pleased smile, said, 'We decided to cut the last ham and I've
fried some tomatoes with it. We've had ours.'

Llewelyn dipped thick squares of home-baked bread in the rich
salty liquor and ate with relish. His mother watched until he gave
a yumming sound, the customary recognition he knew she was
waiting for, after which she returned to her book. He wiped his
plate clean with a piece of bread, drained the last of the sweet

cocoa which his mother had poured and leaned back against the raffia sampler which covered the wall behind.

A movement in the corner drew his eye. Butterpaws was stretching on her back and her belly showed huge with kitten. Ba turned her over and gently eased her off her lap until she fell on to the hearthrug using her claws on the black apron to break her descent. The old lady reached slowly into the released pocket of her skirt and withdrew a small object which caught a gleam from the firelight and Llewelyn recognised the crab apple he had given his grandmother the previous day. She could no more have eaten it than the lump of glass with the reluctant snowstorm inside, bought at the Crystal Palace Exhibition by her mother, but she began to nuzzle and turn it against her faded lips, savouring its redolent smoothness. Eighty-five years old, she was over nine times her grandson's age.

Llewelyn wriggled out, reached up to the little bookcase which Schoolin had made and set into the stone wall of the kitchen to hold his son's *Children'. Encyclopedias*, carried the brimming volume to the sofa with its red plush and peeling braid, and propped the book against his knees.

Butterpaws leapt on his stomach, light as a wren despite her bulging load, caressing his chin with whiskers, purr and fur. Wanting nothing except a piece of Nana's weekly home-made toffee, which was finished anyhow, he began savouring the familiar titles, 'The Man Who Gave His Fortune To Be Remembered For All Time'; 'The Most Soldierly Figure on Earth But a Nobody'; 'Why do I Laugh and Cry?' He started to read the tale of Rip Van Winkle until the warmth of the fire and the ticking stillness of the room, lulled him to sleep.

He opened his eyes to the sound of blurred voices and the sensation of a heavy weight being moved off his stomach.

'Come on, Llew, time for bed. I've lit the Little Lamp,' Nana said. He heard his mother say, 'Carry him to bed, Jack,' and suddenly he was borne aloft in Schoolin's strong arms and the smell of Welsh tweed filled his world. He lay in bed yawning like a tiny hippopotamus as Nana said, 'I'll leave the lamp on the landing until you're asleep,' and tiptoed away.

Llewelyn awoke to find Nana touching his shoulder, the Little Lamp in her hand.

Fingers to lips, she whispered, 'I'm going to do the chimney, it's six o'clock. Would you like to help?'

Llewelyn nodded, his eyes suddenly wide with excitement.

What Nana had in mind was unnecessary in the village cottages, for Schoolin's was one of only five houses which burned coal. The other fires used sootless culm, the fine-grained anthracite dust which was mixed with moistened yellow clay and much cheaper.

Soot removal was the business which had brought Nana from her bed, though not for her the nonsense of 'chimney sweeping'. She had a more effective remedy, and now Llewelyn got out of bed, released the spring-loaded black blind, slowing its noisy ascent with both hands to ensure silence. Above the Squire's trees he could see bars of the fire in the sky over Samson's Quoit. There was no sign of life in the road, though the Indian Game cockerels had begun to greet the new day in Schoolin's poultry shed.

Llewelyn stepped lightly down the stairs, careful to avoid the 'creaker' and joined Nana in the kitchen. With deft strokes she was

cleaning ashes from the grate. Now she reached for a pile of old *Western Mails*, crumpling them into loose balls, pushing them up the chimney as though loading a cannon, with the long, knob-ended poker made by the village smith.

'Now,' she said in the conspiratorial whisper reserved for her more dubious activities, 'go out and come and tell me when it's all right.'

Llewelyn ran up the stone steps and gazed at the lifeless chimney. He heard the match being struck and waited with excitement, and a minute later, after a white puff of smoke, the pot began to pour out thick black streamers and showers of sparks. He ran down with the news.

'Nana, it's going lovely. Like a ship's funnel with stars.' As he stood in the doorway, the chimney changed its note to a blend of growl and roar, indicating that the soot had surrendered and was co-operating in its own execution. He returned outside to see a blazing paper ball floating from the chimneypot, soaring like one of the flares from his *Book of the Great War*, and, still burning, waft into the elms, bringing a babel of caws and wings from the rookery.

As though the noise had summoned a genie, a short dark man materialised at Llewelyn's side. Dafydd Moon, the rabbit trapper neighbour, about to set off on his bicycle rounds, had seen the shower of sparks flying round his cottage roof.

'Chimney's on fire,' he called urgently. 'I'll get water. Ladder's over by there.'

Sensing danger to her fiery exorcism, Nana appeared at the door. 'Ah good morning, Mr Moon, up early you are, isn't it?'

Speaking in a firm tone, she pointed to the belching smoke. 'A bit of old paper must have got sucked up the chimney when I was lighting the fire. Nothing to worry about, though.'

'Nothing to worry about,' she repeated with pauses between the words, halting his departure for water. 'There, look at it, dying down already.' Indeed, the black smoke was changing colour, the sparks thinning out and within minutes the melodrama was over. Llewelyn's father lay on, undisturbed, cocooned in flannel, and Llewelyn's mother, though a light sleeper, was a little hard of hearing anyhow.

Llewelyn joined Nana in the kitchen. Now she built her fire, crumpled newspaper, sticks laid in the old enamel jug to soak up a little overnight paraffin, pieces of shiny coal, all placed with practised precision. Within minutes the new fire was blazing, boiling water for tea.

Nana turned as she rose, 'There's a help you are to me. That's the best we've ever done with the soot.'

She gave a little skip, began to hum 'Home Sweet Home' with the expression of one who had been given a gold sovereign.

The kitchen fire was hers and hers alone, and from early morning roar to nightly expiry she controlled it with physician care. Her great panacea was air. If the patient was slightly ailing, she gave it a gentle whiff of wind from her ancient bellows; if – as only rarely happened – the patient showed symptoms of being *in extremis*, she laid a tin tray in front of the bars and stretched a copy of the *Western Mail* across the chimney entrance to provide a cross-fire wind guaranteed to revive the patient, however feeble the spark of life. Throughout the day, as she skipped in and out of the kitchen, she tidied and titivated the hearth with deft quick strokes of a dusky goose's wing and kept the fire pulsing and flaming with affectionate strokes of her knob-ended poker.

Llewelyn sat down to his slices of home-baked brown bread and salty butter, loaded with his mother's blackcurrant jam. Nana ate plain bread and butter but, before beginning, paid her early morning visit to the corner cupboard for the pack of cards with which she now took a look at what the day held for the family.

'I'm going to have one wish,' she said to Llewelyn. 'I've got a feeling it's going to be a very good day for us all. Now you forget all about me and tuck into your breakfast, there's a good boy.'

Shuffling the cards with a dancing motion, she proceeded to remove the veils which obscured the future for disbelieving mortals.

The key was the 'Wish Card', the Nine of Hearts, and for a member of the family to be sited by this bull's eye of happiness set Nana skipping and singing. But proximity to the 'Disappointment Card' – the ominous Nine of Spades – spread an aura of despondency and drove her to shuffle them harder until they moved from the error of their ways, and if they still persisted they were put aside to come to their senses with the words, 'Ugh a fi, the old cards have gone quite dull.'

Llewelyn emerged to a morning with clouds building up over Abermawr. Already he was a dreamer, beginning to see symbols everywhere. Images poured in from his *Children's Encyclopaedias*, the cloud masses became the Battlemented Castles of Giants, Unscalable Everests of the Sky, Mammoth Smoke Streamers from Gigantic Liners Burning Whole Rain Forests in their Roaring Furnaces, the Black Breathing of Cosmic Dragons, the End of the World.

The sound of a voice and the word 'Dammo' drew him from anxious visions. His friend Tusks emerged, carrying a punctured rubber ball and, aiming a mighty kick at it, his right boot went flying down the bank.

'Dammo,' he said again and hopping exaggeratedly on one leg, pretending to be drunk, clambered down to retrieve it and then sat on the school steps to put it on.

The two boys ran down to the well. Llewelyn was carrying the can which his aunt had asked him to fill and bring back immediately, for it was washday and it would save her one journey to the well. Looking back to the house, he noticed the stream of smoke from the purged chimney rising vertically like a jet from the iron chimney of a threshing engine, white as a cloud of lime.

He cupped his lips with his hands and looking round, indicated the smoke with a wink and nod of his head. 'My auntie and me put the chimney on fire this morning at *three* o'clock. The flames were like *hell*.'

'You never done that,' said Tusks, searching for words to match the image which he could only dimly appreciate. 'Your father would give you a *brilliant* 'idin'.'

Llewelyn sank his can in the well and heaved it out. Carrying water was a hard chore but, at last, after centuries of time, it was coming to an end. The notion of easing the arm-aching shoulder-bowing lot of the village may have occurred to the Squire but he had done nothing about it for twenty years, even though for his farthest village tenant it meant a haul of almost a quarter of a mile. But when the Squire died, his heir, a caring, Baptist solicitor, decided to bring water to his tenants.

His water scheme was an elegant concept. The scheme harnessed the fast-flowing water from the well to power its own pump which was sited at the bottom of a six-foot-deep brick pit, which then pushed the water by pipeline up to Samson's Quoit whence it flowed back and supplied the village by gravity. In a curious way, it seemed to join the village more closely together because, from the bottom of its brick-lined home, The Ram gave out a loud rhythmical sound that reverberated through the village like a communal heart beat.

The scheme had its limitations for it did not run to water-closets – they were still three decades away. It even raised grave suspicions in the minds of John John the elderly roadman and his wife, for water inside the dwelling was surely dangerous and they kept it in its rightful place outside the back door.

The engineer who executed the job was also called the ram, a far-seeing choice for he was fond of the girls. He got drunk each Saturday and was remembered particularly for his nasal bawling of

popular songs, especially 'Shepherd of the Hills' and for many moons after his departure, the village juveniles could be heard singing 'Shepherd of the 'ills, I 'ears yer bawling' as they tried unsuccessfully to imitate his cockney intonation and cacophony.

The Parochial Parish Minute for 17 April 1926 written by Schoolin (who was the Parish Council Clerk for the whole of his stay in the village) formally said goodbye to the back-aching chore . . .

'carried unanimously the thanks of the Meeting to
Mr Walter L. Williams for installing in St Nicholas
Village such an excellent water supply'.

Schoolin's house possessed one feature which made it unique in the village. There was a large attic which ran under the eaves right along one end of the house. It lay over the kitchen, from which the warmth of the fire rose comfortingly through the ill-fitting floorboards. But this connection with the real world belonged only to daylight, for as soon as lamps were lit, the rest of the house vanished like a mirage and the attic was agog and agleam with spell-casting treasures washed in by the tides of years.

With darkness falling, Llewelyn took the Little Lamp and mounted the stairs and ensconced himself on a pensioned-off commode. Outside, the wind was rising. Abermawr was beginning to roar, and a flurry of rain beat against the skylight. First, he would examine the secrets of his father's power, which he himself was about to inherit. He rose and leaned over a tea chest draped with a brown blanket, which he lifted to gloat over the treasures.

Here were his father's Tomes, from which he would one day secretly brief himself for spectacular triumphs when he went to Fishguard County School where, known as 'the son of the famous St Nicholas headmaster', he would distribute his father's learning with throwaway ease among awed contemporaries, topping *every* examination list in the whole of Britain. He moved a few of the books of power, rich with coloured maps, circles, squares and parallelograms, with pictures of Llewelyn the last of the Welsh Princes, the illustrated Ballads of the Scottish Minstrels and the magic stories of the Mabinogion.

But what was this? Among the Tomes, unaccountably missed in a hundred rummages, he found tonight a small brown book with cabbalistic gold scrolls. On the cover (also in gold) appeared the words *The Mystery of the Yellow Room* by Gaston Leroux. Inside was Schoolin's name – John Ll. Jones – and with a growing premonition of trespass into a dangerous world, Llewelyn began to read, and within minutes his heart was pumping and pounding, his scalp in an icy hand. For here on page 7 was the statement that *alone in a locked room,* a victim had been murderously attacked and left for *dead.*

For terror-stricken minutes he remained glued to the narrative until suddenly the door opened and blessed safety returned. His aunt stood in the opening, holding in one hand a cracked chamber pot, painted with clusters of red roses. Impossible that she should throw out a receptacle hallowed by years of family secretions, so the attic was about to receive yet another treasure. She reached for a basket behind her.

'Here's a stroke of luck, Llewelyn' she announced brightly. 'The Squire's wife, has sent over a nice lot of apples for keeping. Here, give me a hand and lay them out. We'll use this sheet of newspaper. Isn't that kind of Mrs James. She's a real lady.'

It was indeed largesse, for apple trees were rare in the wind-swept, stony St Nicholas soil and the Squire's and rector's walled gardens had the only two apple orchards in the village.

Llewelyn reached across and took an apple from the basket. It was hard as stone, rough as a wart, brown as a bulrush, a 'Leathercoat' which would keep almost until apples came round again. It had the little wizened face of a centenarian.

'Now, now,' said Nana, wagging an admonitory forefinger and her hand flashed across to repossess the fruit. 'These are not for eating now. They're for *keeping* for apple sauce. Now give me a hand,' and she began to lay the apples on a spread-out copy of the *Echo*.

'There,' she said as she finished, and added firmly, 'I'll just count them now, then we'll know exactly how many we have got, *won't* we?'

With easy cunning, Llewelyn drew Nana's attention from Mrs James's 'Leathercoats' to an object he knew would decoy her down a golden road.

'What's that over by there then, Nana?' he asked, indicating a huge gaudy plume.

'Dear me,' said his happily unsuspecting aunt, 'if it isn't one of the beautiful feathers which used to be worn by your grandmother in one of her hats. Her feathers were famous. Dear me, what a clever woman your grandmother was.'

Apples forgotten, present in eclipse, the needle of reminiscence ran deep in the tuneful groove of family glorification.

Llewelyn knew it by heart, especially how he was a young mirror-image of his great-grandfather, reputedly the Fishguard paragon of agricultural storekeepers, though the feeling of superiority that burgeoned in attic compost quickly withered in the village street.

His aunt came back to present chores with 'I must go and shut up the fowls now. Why don't you take that feather down to your grandmother and ask her about it. Be careful with the Little Lamp, there's a good boy.'

Llewelyn stood for a moment in the shadowy attic, the dream house where household goods mysteriously changed into household gods. He left the plume but took two 'Leathercoats' instead, and carrying the Little Lamp carefully so that it wouldn't flare in the draughts of the opening doors and preceded by Butterpaws, her tail stuck up straight as the school chimney, he went down to his supper of toasted cheese and rice pudding with golden syrup on top, ready to slip the treasure into Ba's old hand when no one was looking.

CHAPTER FOUR

The Dream of Isaiah Jenkins

'The Rector sent some apples to be distributed among the children this afternoon. To show their appreciation the scholars gave three cheers for the Rector.'

Headmaster's Log Book, 7 September 1932

The Reverend Isaiah was the twenty-fifth rector of St Nicholas and it is unlikely this endearingly tiny church, which dates back to the thirteenth century, ever had a more memorable vicar. Brought up on a small Cardiganshire farm until scholarships had taken him to Lampeter Theological College (the national Mecca over the years for the stream of Welsh Church Ordinands), his personality was unforgettable. Six feet tall, heavily built, dark complexioned, with high cheek bones, a low brow, and black hair cropped short, he held one with his piercing brown eyes set in yellowish, faintly blood-streaked whites. His veins were charged with mercury, for he never attained a standstill state, but a sort of stationary dance, and his nearest approach to silence was a running fire of '. . . yes . . . yes . . . yes . . . hm . . . hm . . .' which kept him prepared for his invariably racing getaway. At the same time, he held the ends of his sleeves with opening and closing fingers, keeping his arms away from his body to ensure no fuels leaked away to gravity while his engine was idling. He walked at a furious pace and spoke like an auctioneer at a sale.

As both clergyman and Chairman of the Church School Managers, Isaiah's visits to school were frequent and, as on this Wednesday morning, unannounced. He entered as though blown by a pentecostal wind, slamming the door behind him, scattering exclamations and gestures like a badger digging his sett, but establishing immediate rapport with the children; though his own young son – like Llewelyn, when Schoolin was indulging in class his dreams of hunting duck and trout – was often embarrassed by his father's eccentric style.

At a lift of Schoolin's baton, the children rose to provide the well-rehearsed litany for members of the School Managers.

'Good morning sir, we trust you are very well.'

Gripping his coat sleeves in familiar fashion with a stream of 'Hm . . . yes . . . yes . . . yes . . . very good . . . hm . . .' he listened with a smile and then responded with, 'Thank you, children, very good, very good . . . very polite children . . . a credit to the school, Mr Jones. Hm . . . hm . . . yes . . . yes . . . yes . . .'

When the interval between these interjections lengthened to his equivalent of silence, Schoolin with the gesture of a head waiter announcing a special dish, waved him behind the desk, and opened the Register which Isaiah began to call in a solemn sequence of names. (The Local Education Authority expected all Managers to pay regular visits to the school to call-check the Register and sign it as being correct, and had on numerous occasions complained of the infrequency of the Managerial audit of the Schoolmaster's entries.)

Isaiah used his visits to give a short Scripture lesson and on this day, oblivious of the fact he had interrupted an arithmetic lesson already in progress, he turned to Schoolin.

'I'd like to set the children three little exercises I've made up, Mr Jones, with your permission, of course. And I wondered whether you could write them on the blackboard for the children to copy into their copy books. And don't write down the answers, ha . . . ha . . . hm . . . hm . . .'

His round face split in a smile of tobacco-stained teeth, and he rolled his brown eyes at the delighted children. He handed Schoolin a small sheet of paper on which Schoolin read three riddles.

1. What did Adam and Eve give their children which they never had themselves? (Answer = Parents)
2. What has man seen that God hasn't? (Answer = One greater than himself)
3. What is there that God never saw? (Answer = One as great as Himself)

Schoolin copied the holy riddles on to the blackboard and instructed the children to write the questions in their writing books, and to bring the answers the following day. (To Isaiah's subsequent delight three children – or perhaps their parents – got them right.)

Isaiah concentrated on the Old Testament because this was safe ground for church and chapel alike, since matters such as Holy Communion were inflammatory, especially as there was a rumour that churches were about to desert God's own home-baked bread for some heathenish, papish things called 'round wafers'. Isaiah also chose stories with which he could point to a moral at the end.

'And do you know what happened to those naughty children who shouted 'Go up thou baldhead' to the prophet Elijah? Does anybody know? No? Well, I'll tell. They were eaten by *bears* . . .' (a pause here and a waggling forefinger) '. . . so always be good children and show respect to your fathers and mothers, and', he added as though he had just remembered 'to Mr Jones . . .'

Although he had no difficulty in holding the children's attention, their answers did not always match their interest. After describing the betrayal of the shorn Samson by Delilah, Isaiah confidently asked little elfin-faced Mary Beynon, who had been hanging on his every word, 'So how did Samson lose his strength then, Mary dear?'

'Please sir, that wicked 'ooman with long air cut off 'is 'ead.'

'Tut, tut,' said Isaiah, 'you haven't been listening properly, have you?'

But his favourite story was Goliath and David, a country boy with a marksman's eye as good as his own and when he reached

the stone-slinging part which toppled the giant, he could barely contain his enthusiasm in front of the grinning children, as he accompanied his narrative with a gleeful spray of 'hm . . . hm . . . goodness me . . . what a shot . . . what a *beauty* . . .', shaking himself like a black retriever getting rid of water. The children waited for this with delighted anticipation and were never disappointed.

Several times each year, the Reverend showed his affection by sending the children apples from his orchard.

Isaiah's loves after his little church and the children, were vegetable growing, shooting and fishing. He grew (and gave away in the course of visiting sick and old parishioners) huge-hearted cabbages, hernia-threatening marrows, onions the size of cricket balls and – with the enthusiasm of mission – exhorted farmers to deliver manure to the vicarage as though laying up treasure in heaven. This he piled into barrows, black and rich as plum puddings. He always had soil in his trouser bottoms and even on the Lord's day frequently gave out a whiff of manure. He held three services every Sunday, alternating the times between his two parish churches, though it was at St Nicholas Evensong that he gave his congregation best value for money.

His winter services, for which wind and rain and sea often provided a backcloth, remain in the memory. When the stone-rolling Abermawr tide roared in the village darkness and the sound

of the church bell was only intermittently heard before being
blown away, the hat-clutching faithful had to lean hard against the
blast to reach the church porch, where first lift of the stiff latch
brought the waiting smith to hold open the door (never more than
half ajar though) with his brawny arm. Even so, it was difficult to
avoid a spurt of flame and smoke from the hanging lamps, and the
stoves hissing in the aisle. Evening worship had its own smell of
paraffin (heightened sporadically by the draught-flared wicks), pew
oak polished to mirror shine by Dora the cleaner (whose husband
was declining lingeringly to a consumptive's grave) and a faint
odour of mustiness from the damp West wall.

The singing was dominated by the rector's wife's big contralto.
She sang the responses and hymns while playing the harmonium
(from which Schoolin's wife had been ousted, much to her dudgeon
and Schoolin's embarrassment), attempting perhaps to compensate
for her husband's lack of vocal timbre, for Isaiah's intonation was
the voice equivalent of Epsom Salts. Her contralto was
complemented by Schoolin's harmonising baritone – he harmonised
as naturally as he walked – and by the rather harsh bass of the
smith.

Isaiah's most memorable sermons were inspired by his namesake,
especially when he preached on the prophet's dream of the peaceful
kingdom. As he got into his oracular sing-song stride, he entered
a private dream world, where his voice and hands wrought magic
with the species: so that eagle and partridge perched side by side
on the crag, otter played hide and seek with the trout, the fox gave
dawn duets with the cockerel, the rabbit and weasel, the hawk and
the field mouse were all pals together; so that there was no more
killing, which, as the less poetic members of the congregation
sometimes thought, was a bit odd when you remembered that
Isaiah spent all his spare time in the winter months shooting
everything edible on land and in the air that came within range of
his twelve-bore gun. He hardly ever missed.

In any case, if Isaiah failed, it was likely the figure by his side
would make good the error. For no village sported a more deadly
pair than Schoolin and Isaiah Jenkins. For almost two decades,
they scurried together over moor and fen, crags, ditch and torrent
with the schoolmaster half a pace behind, often hard put to keep
up with Isaiah's longer legs – quartering the country like a pair of
truffle hounds on the scent.

The rector wore a battered porkpie hat, the schoolmaster a
disreputable trilby, both squashed well down to put their faces in

shadow – especially during the game shooting season because neither had a special licence, and though they shot game with the connivance of the farmers, there was still the potential menace of the heel-peddling bobby from Mathry. Throughout the season, they wore ankle-length raincoats, pockets opened into strengthened linings to serve as containers for the dead creatures – partridge, pheasant, curlew, snipe, plover, woodcock, duck, teal, rabbit; or from a different medium – crab, lobster, trout, eel, sewin. These they tumbled on to their respective tables with thigh-slapping glee. Schoolin's poacher's pocket stank like a mix of holt and den, and from time to time when cleansing gales were blowing, his wife Catherine turned it inside out, and hung it out on the backyard clothes line to sweeten.

So it is not surprising that although Isaiah was famous for sermons and gardening, it was his prowess as a sportsman that is recalled in the village today, either by those who personally knew him or those who, down the years, have listened to tales that gathered like moss round his name. Yet one of his more memorable exploits remained unknown in the parish except to Schoolin and his son who became involved in the happening almost by accident. The site of the event was the Squire's pond.

Ponds were widespread features of the countryside in those days. Every farm, indeed every country house of any size and consequence, had its own, and the ponds could be as distinct as the personalities of their owners. On the farms, they were watering places for horses and dairy cows which drank their fill twice a day as they moved in and out of the milking byres. During the twenties and early thirties when duck eggs were more popular with the St Nicholas housewives than the eggs of the domestic hen (until the salmonella scare of the thirties brought them into disrepute), they were pin-money earners for the farmers' wives, as well. The ducks on the farm ponds were all Khaki Campbells, bright-eyed light brown laying machines which lived in the water, except when they came in to lay or to guzzle their barley meal.

The Squire's pond too had once been a working stretch of water, storing and releasing power for the Oak Grange water wheel which turned the millstones for the Squire's mill. In 1929, he decided to drain and stock his pond with rainbow trout fry. The emptied site disclosed a foot of black mud into which sows from the village smallholding were turned for a slobbering harvest of eel. The cleaned pond was left for a few weeks before the fry were brought in, and over the unfished years the tiny rainbows had grown big and brilliantined and bountiful, leaping for flies in the evening light in a manner marvellous to behold. Isaiah wore knowledge of this teeming larder literally within a few casts of the rectory like a nettle-tipped hairshirt.

History provides many examples of men of God succumbing to temptation. The agents of fall have been divers – drink, gluttony, possessions, power and pride. But for Isaiah – whose upbringing on that impoverished Cardiganshire farm and the need to exploit to the limit all free victuals on the ground, in the water, or on the wing, had left him with an insatiable itch to plunder the countryside – it was trout.

On this Thursday evening, when virtually the whole village was attending a nearby Fair and the Oak Grange was also empty, he could mortify the flesh no longer and his dark-clad figure hurried in a wide detour through the village fields with an unmistakable air of furtiveness.

With fireman despatch, he climbed the iron ladder to the pond, which was raised to provide the fall for the mill stream, put his rod together, baited the hook with a fat pink worm and made his first cast. Whereas he normally cast with authority and style, savouring a fluent technique, he was content now with a poacher's underarm fling. His urgency seemed to carry to the fish, and as though driven by some sort of death wish, within half an hour, eleven fat beauties were inside the canvas bag. Eleven, boyo, boyo. What a catch, what a joy. Only one more for a round dozen and he would call it a day and nobody would ever know. Isaiah made a last cast and once again, the bait was taken, the taut line reeled in, the fish netted, bagged. He disjointed his rod, picked up the bag, and turned to leave, when, without warning, the clods and stones gave way at the pond edge and with his legs as straight as a clerical tailor's dummy, he slid into the water.

Isaiah's feet touched bottom at about sixty inches which left him just able to breathe. For a moment, the cold drove out all thought until the shock of his predicament seared his brain. He must get out. He scrabbled at the wall. But there was no handhold. He was going to have to wade, so he moved his right foot tentatively but found he could not touch bottom. He tried with his left. The pond was deeper all round him. He could not swim, what could he do? Panic rose. He would be unfrocked, or he would drown. The choice was clear . . .

'Help,' he shouted in the stentorian which had made his sermons famous. 'Help, help . . . I'm drowneding . . .'

It was providential that Schoolin, never a one for fairs, was home, and even more so that he was up a ladder cleaning the upstairs windows in the front of the School House.

'Help! Help!' the bellow came again and this time obviously from the direction of the Squire's pond. Schoolin came down, ran toward the pond like an elderly greyhound, and clambered up the iron ladder. His son Llewelyn followed.

'Goodgodlemighty, it's the rector!' cried Schoolin. 'What the devil are you doing there, Isaiah?' and then as he took in the situation, he called urgently, 'Hold on while I fetch a ladder.'

Llewelyn stared at the man of God in the pond, his parson's collar just visible, water lying in the brim of his papal hat, arms outstretched, fingers clawing the loose stone of the pond wall. He was awed at the sight of a rector in such a pickle and to cover his embarrassment, he picked up the bag.

'Put that down, boy. Put that d-d-down I say,' Isaiah said immediately in chattering tones.

Blushing, he obeyed, as Schoolin arrived with the rescue ladder which he lowered carefully between the rector's outstretched arms

C

and, with the help of Schoolin's steadying hand, Isaiah rose from the water, streaming like a colander, his face white as flour.

'Jack, Jack,' he said, 'I'm so grateful . . . so grateful you heard me.' Then the rector surfaced for a moment. 'You are my saviour. I could have been unfrocked,' he said, with a gasping intake of breath.

'You'd better come to my house at once,' said Schoolin, 'and get dried.' But looking round with goggle-eyed caution, Isaiah shook his head, and with a hoarse 'God bless you, Jack. Tell your boy to keep his mouth shut', descended the ladder, clutching the bag and rod, and skulked like a fox to the rectory.

The following day, Schoolin received five trout, wrapped and carefully tied in the centre spread of the *Church Times*. The wages of sin, fried in salty Welsh butter, were delicious.

Isaiah was able to forgo publicity for this episode for Schoolin and his son stayed mum, but he made no attempt to do so on another fishing occasion which earned him fame and placed him among local angling giants. His name still stands in Fishguard as the angler who caught the biggest trout ever with a fly and won a spanking new rod, though it was in truth a juicy worm from Isaiah's dungheap which tempted and finally took the six-pound Trout of Cleddau. The old cannibal had taunted anglers for years in his sanctuary under the bridge until Isaiah hooked him with that worm.

'Tut, tut,' he said to Schoolin with poacher logic, when the latter, with some misgiving, agreed to sign his name as witness to the fly which Isaiah had supposedly used for the record-breaking catch, 'don't worry, Jack, don't worry, my old boy. What's the difference, fly or worm. Purely nominal, a matter of technique. It's the fish that matters after all. Don't you agree . . . hm . . . hm . . . hm . . .'

Isaiah brought a new English word into currency in the parish vocabulary – donation. In the first weeks after his arrival, one of his chief tasks as Chairman of the School Managers was to help with the clearing of a £400-debt for repairs and rebuilding in the school. For while coal, shovels, lavatory buckets, disinfectant,

piano tuning, desk repairs and other day-to-day sundries were eligible for grant, all additions or renovations to the building proper had to be paid for by major bursts of fund raising from church and parish. So Schoolin and Isaiah had to go on a begging spree, and over a period of two months raised a total of £132, mostly from the Fishguard tradesmen. To find the remainder, it was decided to hold an Autumn Fair in the rectory grounds.

For one person in the village, church fêtes and fairs had a special significance. Miss Ruth Morgan, the blacksmith's sister, was a middle-aged dwarf hunchback with a head like a pumpkin and a shy stricken smile. She lived with and looked after her father, the old retired smith who, with a progressively slowing gait, walked each day, until the week before his death, to the smithy where he sat on a sack-clothed baulk of elm, one shoulder-of-mutton arm resting on the handle of the old pensioned-off bellows, his complexion a dark teak, his beard grizzled as though some of the smoke of the half century he had worked in the forge had been trapped in the hairs. His cloth cap, greasy as a black goose's skin, perched on the back of his head. They made a quaint pair, seated by the fire at night, this retired Tubal Cain and his dwarf daughter, the social highlight of whose life was the weekly visit by Schoolin's sister-in-law to regale her with the latest episodes from the *Family Herald* serials. The trials and tribulations of the aristocratic Lady Verinder and the machinations of Count Fosco were matters of grave concern to this little Jenny Wren, and Nana, the ideal storyteller, was so bound up with her own performance that there was no call for the audience to be shy.

Ruth earned her few pounds not from making new going-out clothes but principally from the making of flannel petticoats and knickers, pinafores and aprons. Her father contributed his old age pension, and several times a week Martha, the blacksmith's wife, brought down a saucepan of the strong Welsh broth for which she was famous in the parish. Ruth never went out and her windows and front door stayed fast shut summer and winter and though her brother was a church warden, and she was 'strong church', she never attended services but had communion brought to her 'once a quarter' by the rector.

But she came into her very special own when the shops in Fishguard, having given their donations to the school, were again canvassed by Schoolin and Isaiah scrounging for lengths of cotton cloth, remnants of velvet and serge, bits of flannel and leatherette, tape, elastic and reels of cotton, from which the indefatigable dwarf

fashioned aprons for grown-ups, pinafores for little girls, caps for little boys, velvet pinpads, needle cases and coloured chair cushions to shine in the culm-fire gloaming. Ruth's stall was always the belle of any fair.

There were many others: a coconut shy – the coconuts donated by Bilbow the grocer – which Schoolin, with his barker's stentorian, agreed to man; a stall looked after by Meiriog the blacksmith, where one threw iron quoits at a peg in the ground; a weight-guessing stall with a weaner pig prize, and one for throwing darts at playing cards. There was a home-made wine and toffee stall supplied by Schoolin's wife and Nana; a stall for jams and jellies and chutneys from the rector's wife (whose sick mother prevented her attending the event); a raffle in which first prize was a live Michaelmas goose and finally a fortune-telling tent, a pitch to which Nana laid firm claim despite schoolin's strong private opposition. His reservations about his sister-in-law had nothing to do with her Delphic techniques but were inspired by fears about her outrageous outspokenness. Nana could, virtually without trying, make the best-endowed saint run out of cheeks.

'I wish you'd try and head off your sister from this fortune-telling business, Catherine,' Schoolin kept saying to his wife in the weeks before the Autumn Fair. 'You know what she is. She's sure to offend somebody. Mrs Beynon only meant the fortune-telling business as a joke. But Nana's taking it seriously.'

'Jack, dear,' came the reply, 'you know Nana, too. Once she gets an idea, wild horses won't stop her. She really believes in those old cards.'

So it was that the name of Madame Crystal (Nana's own choice) was painted on a piece of orange box by the young village carpenter (whose spectacles flashed red in the setting sunlight as he worked his plane with the regularity of a loom in his tiny workshop) and Nana's closet was joined on to the tiny entertainment township which had mushroomed in the autumn sunlight.

The rectory lawn looked trim and green and inviting as Mrs Davies arrived from the Big House in the neighbouring parish and descended rather falteringly from the gleaming governess car driven by her daughter, to perform what was to be her last ceremony at the end of a life devoted to public service.

'Good afternoon, Mr Jenkins,' she greeted Isaiah as she stepped on to the rectory terrace.

In ankle-length sealskin coat, Queen Mary toque, three-quarter face veil, and resting gloved hands on a polished silver-handled blackthorn stick like a wand of high office, she was every inch the grande dame exuding graciousness and style. With a faintly sheepish Isaiah by her side, she surveyed the attendance benignly through her lorgnette.

'I am very pleased to be here on this beautiful day,' she said in a Lady Bracknell voice with the faintest hint of quaver, 'for I always think the autumn is the most beautiful part of the year. We are here today to spend our money in a good cause. Money is short

everywhere, for greed and the call for equality are threatening to
impoverish our dear country. But ours is still a very tolerant
nation and our church school, built mainly from church funds, is
open to all, regardless of creed. But it is the duty of us all to help
meet the cost of repairs if the children of our parishes are to be
properly educated. I don't propose to say any more, or to keep you
from your enjoyment. So have a good time, all of you. Spend your
money freely. It is an excellent cause. I have considerable
pleasure in declaring this Church Fair open.'

Close by, Nana listened, holding with ostentation her badges of
office, two new packs of playing cards and, for no ascertainable
reason, the Book of Common Prayer. She had an almost religious
regard for the aristocracy and was a walking encyclopaedia of
information on High Family Trees and their Branches, and
Mrs Davies' ancestry went back a long way.

The Autumn Fair would have yielded a poor return had
attendance been restricted to the village and the parish, but there
was an infusion of money from a contingent of loyal Fishguard
churchgoers who arrived by charabanc. Not merely did they swell
the crowd but the presence of new faces and the warmth generated
by this evidence of outside support and solidarity produced the
good will and enthusiasm which makes events of this kind go with
a swing.

The beginning of the fun of the fair was punctuated by Schoolin, barking a little self-consciously but in his best far-carrying baritone.

'Coconuts, three shies a penny . . . your luck is in today . . .' and then falling into the well-tried proverb, 'Three tries for a Welshman.'

Then the buying spree began, with the Reverend Isaiah bustling from stall to stall, waving his arms, spreading the spirit of goodwill with unending streams of 'good . . . very good . . . excellent . . . yes . . . yes . . . hm . . . hm . . .' The Fishguard contingent, which included a number of well-breached tradesmen, bought generously and without too much discrimination. The people from the parish concentrated expressly on the useful articles, especially on the clothes and sundries from Miss Ruth Morgan's stall, which did the best business of all.

Meanwhile at the end of the row of stalls, Schoolin's sister-in-law had taken possession of her little sentry box. She found her task easy. For those customers who were known to her only by name, she had recourse to the well-tried formulae of dark men and journeys across water, playing a game in which she was well versed, from her addiction to novelettes and the *Family Herald*. For those whose present condition and history she well knew, she could provide, as it were, better value for money. And local business was brisk, which was hardly surprising, for with the present mostly a harsh day to day reality, the notion that the future might hold something different, even golden, was a strong reason for three escapist pennyworth, even in fun.

Despite Schoolin's anxieties, Nana's afternoon of encounters had given no real offence to anybody. But towards the close when the winner of the goose raffle was announced, the *enfant terrible*, as he had feared, ousted the oracle. Nana had emerged from her closet to fetch herself a cup of tea, to a sound of clapping and cheering. It greeted the news that the Reverend Isaiah had bought the winning ticket for the green goose. Proudly he scooped up his prize, and with the wings pinioned in his strong countryman's arms did a laughing lap of honour round the fair, moving eventually in the direction of Madame Crystal's pitch.

She watched his approach with rising dudgeon. No prize for the Jones family in the raffle after all. A word about cheating – she could not quite remember it – which Gwilym Lloyd George used at an election meeting in the St Nicholas schoolroom – it sounded something like 'chick canary' – came briefly into her mind, for Nana's belief that all edible raffle prizes belonged by a sort of

Divine Right to her family, was so fierce that she was almost capable of accusing God of cheating.

Isaiah arrived, bubbling and boisterous. 'Ah, good afternoon, Miss Acraman,' he began as he entered her closet and sat down, 'been meaning to come and see you. How are we making out then? Hm . . . hm . . . very good . . . very good . . . You'll see I've brought my feathered Ventry Loquist with me to have her fortune told ha . . . ha . . . very nice goose indeed. Mrs Jenkins will be very pleased. Such a pity her mother is ill and prevented her being here today. Now then, let's see what the future holds. Plenty of rabbits and pheasants I hope and good crops in the garden. Hm . . . hm . . . he . . . ha . . . very good.'

But Nana was not to be wooed from her priorities by any amount of winner's eloquence. Looking at Isaiah over her glasses, she pointed with a mixture of severity and reproach at the captive in his arms.

'Dear me, Mr Jenkins,' she began, 'do you think it was wise of you to allow yourself to win that goose, with you so soon in the parish. I don't think if I was a vicar and just *induced*, I would think it wise to win a goose. Makes people think it's cheating, doesn't it?'

Before the open-mouthed Isaiah could react with speech, she seized the cards, and without shuffling began her prophecies.

'Dear me, dear me,' she said, the ostrich feather in her flowerpot hat bobbing in sympathetic surprise, 'it looks as though you're going to get some more good luck as well as a goose. Couldn't be money though, could it, because I heard you came from a very poor family.'

Before the astonished Isaiah could reply, she was off again, dancing the cards in her two hands.

'Ah! Oh dear me. That's better. I mean, tut tut. This looks quite nasty. Not good at all. See here, Mr Jenkins,' – she turned the cards slightly towards him – 'here's a big building, must be a church I suppose and look, here's the King of Hearts, must be Bishop Prosser of St Davids, I suppose – he's a sort of *King*, isn't he, *and* he's fair – and I'm sorry to have to tell you that you and he are surrounded by all spades, all nasty old spades. Oh drat me, here's that awful Old Nine of Spades himself.'

Nana looked up with an expression of arch concern.

'I hope you're not in serious trouble with the bishop,' she finished brightly.

'But let's try again,' she said, running the cards together with more anti-Isaiah prophecies bubbling in her mind when the seance was brought to a premature close with a great pother and clatter of wings as the goose escaped from Isaiah's clasp, which had been progressively weakened as his future was unfolded.

Restored to reality by the threat of losing his prize, he rushed out flapping his arms in pursuit, scattering exclamations of woe like confetti. With a fine display of wing-aided speed and giving out a loud continuous cackling the goose ran down the drive, making for the road. Schoolin dashed to close the gate, and with half the fair now in pursuit, the goose dodged in and out of the trees before being eventually coralled in the coconut shy. Isaiah marched with his captive to the rectory stable and shut her in. The little drama provided just the right note of fun to induce a last spurt of spending (though there were no more visitors to the Delphic closet) and when the takings were counted up that night, the total revealed a princely sum of £70, which with donations solicited from far and wide plus a grant of £50 from the Bishop's fund, was eventually brought up to £400.

There were to be other Autumn Fairs during Schoolin's and Isaiah's partnership but there was never again any more fortune-telling. Schoolin often experienced difficulty in heading off his

sister-in-law from her dubious initiatives but would have been sorely tempted to bring his strong arm into the argument if Nana had threatened another session of prophecy, especially after he heard her say to his wife, 'Ugh a fi, fancy winning that goose. I gave Isaiah a real bit of what for, before the old thing flew down and spoilt everything.'

Isaiah, fortunately, took a tolerant view. 'Jack, Jack,' he said, 'if you don't mind my saying so, what a case your Miss Acraman is. Do you know, she almost accused me of fiddling the raffle prize! Me, a clergyman of the Disestablished Church of Wales. Tut, tut. With an imagination like that, she ought to write a book. Yes, indeed, she should write a book, hm . . . hm . . . ha . . . ha . . . he . . . he . . .' and he began to laugh, holding out his sleeves, his laughter echoed by matching bellows from the relieved Schoolin.

Isaiah forgave, the school debt was paid and, as many times before, Miss Ruth's little stall had made a major contribution to church and school funds. On the following Monday, when the new issue of the *Family Herald* arrived, with the last exciting chapter of 'The Moonstone', Nana walked along to Ruth's house in the evening and, at her sister's request, took the dressmaker a jug of fresh cream purchased from Spring Gardens Farm. She knocked at the door and then as usual turned the knob to enter but the door was locked. She knocked again, and minutes later slow footsteps dragged along the hall, the key was turned and the old smith stood in the doorway. He made a gesture, inviting Nana inside and preceded her into Ruth's little workroom. The dwarf was sitting in the gloom, staring ahead, her hands resting on her treadle machine.

Nana put down the jug of cream which was immediately seized and Ruth poured it down her throat without drawing breath. That was the first the village knew that Ruth had developed 'drinking diabetes' of which she died three months later.

CHAPTER FIVE

Heresies and Hosannas

*'Llangloffan Baptist Preaching Service. School
closed for the day.'*

Headmaster's Log Book, 16 May 1923

If St Nicholas Church is very small, the village chapel is tiny.
It is a satellite of the big Baptist tabernacle of Llangloffan and in
the days before cars made the three-mile journey easy, it was a
thriving centre of village worship, though it never rated a minister.
The services revolved round a trio of deacons: William Davis of
Spring Gardens Farm, David Evans, Clogs' father and, above all,
John John, rabbit trapper and part-time roadman.

John was a medium tall, fiercely moustachioed man of mild
disposition, with a specially long stride. Each stride was
accompanied by a tiny head nod, as though he were pacing
distances, an impression heightened by his habit of staring at the
ground as he walked. His principal leisure activities were mixing
culm, reading the Bible in the candle-lit gloaming of his tiny
cottage, and praying in chapel.

75

John was thus a natural chapel leader (apart from the fact he possessed a fine quartet of tuning forks for guiding pitch at the harmoniumless meetings). He was also a powerful debater and had at least once held his own in an argument with Bilbow, the slippery atheist village grocer, on a tricky point of fundamentalist theology.

The matter had come to a head when a travelling menagerie visited nearby Fishguard, with lions, tigers, an elephant and three apes. John, like the able-bodied rest of the village, cycled in to see the show and after staring at the caged trio of apes for a long time, decided the shopkeeper's derisive claim that the entire population of St Nicholas was descended from monkeys was not merely blasphemously untrue, but also bestial, carnal as well as downright insulting, and that something had to be done about it.

John engaged Bilbow and his much-quoted scientific friends, Wells and Huxley, almost by chance, one Saturday evening just before closing time, when he called in with fellow deacon, the carter David Evans, for their weekly purchase of Shag.

Bilbow, who was bored and felt like some fun, provided the opening gambit. 'Well, gents bach,' he said with a provocative smile. 'Have you been to see the monkeys? Hey? Funny to think we come from such as them. Hey? None of that Adam and Eve nonsense, hey?'

Completely out of his depth, David stared straight ahead and held his peace. But John felt the moment had arrived to bear witness and prepared to launch the missiles which were to demolish or at least dent the heresies of the Darwinian grocer.

'You says, Bilbow, that the Bible isn't true. You says that Adam and Eve never was in no garden. You says we comes down from the monkeys. Why don't you just look around you, mun? Don't men look now the same as they always 'ave looked. 'Aven't you seen the pictures of men from hundreds of years ago? *They* don't look like no monkeys. They look the same as us, though they wore collars. Don't they, Bilbow? Don't they look the same? If what you say is true, then your own grandfather must 'ave looked more like a monkey than you do, Bilbow. Did 'e, Bilbow? Did your grandfather look more like a monkey? Eh?' Then, as though the thought had only just occurred, he added with a sly grin, 'Perhaps 'e did, Bilbow, perhaps 'e did. Perhaps that's the trouble.'

Astonished by the power of John's logic, the shopkeeper, faced with unthinkable surrender to a rabbit trapper, had immediate recourse to the always available shoal of red herrings which could reduce any debate to a shambles, and stand any idea on its head.

'Ah John, ah John,' he said with a waggling finger, 'I'll ask you just one question about what you have just said. Have you read the *Science of Life* and the writings of Bishop Barnes? No? I thought you hadn't, I thought you hadn't or – if you don't mind my saying so, John bach – you wouldn't talk such bloody rubbish.'

Then a real decider came into Bilbow's mind and he leaned forward with a triumphant grin, 'Tell me,' he said, 'now tell me, what *language* did your so-called Adam and Eve speak among those old apples?'

John thought deeply for a moment, brushing the ends of his walrus moustache with the thumbs and forefingers of both hands. 'I think they spoke in Welsh,' he said.

Honours were even.

Like all true missionaries, John John believed in sowing seeds in the young, and had his own special method of preparing the soil. As Llewelyn and Tusks watched him mixing his culm that night – five of anthracite dust to one of wetted clay by volume – mortaring the mix with finicky precision, he hitched up his yellow corduroy trousers, 'yorked' just below the knee with binder twine, to keep his legs warm, and said, 'I hopes you boys will be coming to the prayer meeting tonight?'

He looked craftily at Llewelyn. 'There's peardrops for them as does, Llewelyn . . .'

That night at seven o'clock, the congregation of true believers was swollen by a shifty apostate, the first of many subsidised attendances. In the absence of William Davis, John was cast in the role of evening praying star. Though he experienced difficulty in getting into stride if he chewed too much tobacco before the meeting, because it made him tipsy, tonight inspiration flowed without pause or delay and after an eloquent talk with the Almighty in Welsh, he announced he would regale Him with a short spell of English prayer. His choice of subject was appropriate.

'Oh, my friends,' he called, 'consider God's conies. Tell me. What is the conies? What is the conies?' he repeated.

'Is conies lions and tigers chasing the little deers in Hafrica and Hindia? No, my friends, not that, not that . . .

'Is conies helephants shouting and tramplying through the jungle? No, my friends, not that, not that.

'Is conies hapes? No no, my friends, not hapes. Not hapes.

'Is conies cannibals that eats men? No no, my friends, not that, not that.' John's rhetoric might have gone on a lot longer as he savoured the unusual sound of his English bestiary, but though there was universal respect for his religious status, signs of impatience began to appear on the faces of his listeners and John noticed a conspicuous absence of the approving 'Amens' which he particularly relished, as he prayed, from his comrades in the Big Seat. So he brought his prayer to an abrupt end with the words, 'No no, my friends, conies is just God's little rabbits, put on earth specially for the trappers to catch.'

Grimacing as he rose, he ran his fingers through his moustache, announced the title of the last hymn and, selecting the appropriate tuning fork, struck it with more force than strictly necessary against the edge of the pew so that the Middle 'C' went pinging with extra reverberation through the harmoniumless chapel.

The sharp division of the village on Sundays into church and chapel was real enough, but there was one Sunday in the year when church people openly joined an event organised by the Baptist deacons. The Llangloffan chapel held its annual tea-party on Abermawr beach, an appropriate venue, because a former Llangloffan member, William Lewis, had lived nearby and written some Baptist hymns which are nationally famous and are celebrated on brass plaques on his chapel walls. Even Schoolin's sister-in-law, for whom 'chapel' had a common connotation, had been known to eat a Baptist bun on these occasions, safe from Baptist contagion in the salt-laden Atlantic ozone of Abermawr.

Llewelyn rode down in William Davis's trap, the big kettles and cans for tea-making, rattling and jumping under the seat. Horse and trap crunched slowly into the cool twilight of the lane to the beach, and pulled up where a screen of polygonum, old man's beard, honeysuckle and tall thin soaring saplings hid the Little Well, surrounded by stones and gleaming like a gem in a mossy, hart's-tongue setting. Cans filled, they rattled off to the beach.

Abermawr appeared suddenly, a lit stage of blue and white, a beach of two faces, the sea near the entrance dour and menacing even in high summer, the waves in the lea of the Muntan promontory, creaming over golden sand, wide and welcoming. The waters were kept at bay by a tide-fleeing bastion of stones, entailing an awkward passage across the pebbles, which had long engulfed the old road. Some well-known figures had arrived and Mr Davis, as senior deacon present, allocated responsibilities. He singled out a frail, white-bearded figure leaning on a stick, a pillar of the Temperance movement.

'Hello, Mr Pugh, how nice and early you are. You're waiting to go across. This is young Llewelyn Jones, Jones the Schoolin's son. You'll be quite safe with him, he'll help you, he's Major Willie Acraman's nephew, you know. . . .'

Mr Pugh had known Llewelyn's uncle in his roistering Fishguard youth as the boss and hero of the young bucks (though warned off perhaps by the example of a father who had poured thousands of pounds worth of booze down his own and numerous toadying throats, his Uncle Willie later became a strict teetotaller).

Llewelyn took up his stance by the old man, and felt a predatory finger close round his upper arm with a painful grip.

After a few uncertain steps, Mr Pugh paused and said, 'Dear me, what's happened to your arm then? It's like a stick of rhubarb. He! He!' Then conscious that the joke was against himself, he added anxiously, 'You sure you can hold me?'

As his confidence grew he returned to his subject.

'They tell me you're Major Willie Acraman's nephew then,' he went on. 'You'll have to eat up if you want to be like him, won't you? You don't drink, do you? He didn't, you know.'

He stopped for a moment, stared craftily into Llewelyn's eyes as though he expected to find a glass of whisky under his eyelids. Then his mind hopped to another subject.

He took a long look at the pebbly, road-eclipsing barrier,

squinting painfully in the strong sunlight. 'Where's the road gone, then?' he began to complain. 'I used to drive a horse and cart to the Muntan twenty years ago. Where's it gone to now, and how do they bring in the lime. Oh dear, dear me, there's a sorry state of affairs, isn't it?'

He worked his way across the bastion of stones, increasingly in the past and, greatly relieved to have delivered him, Llewelyn escaped and joined in carrying driftwood for the kettle-boiling fires. The mountains of currant buns, hillocks of Welsh cakes, headlands of bread and butter, with jam and cheese, were brought across in square baskets of gleaming white willow.

Then the guzzling and drinking and stone-throwing began; women paddled in ice-cold suds washing up knickered thighs, tide-honed flat stones went skimming and leaping or died in the walls of the breaking combers – the left-handed Gwilym Thomas, eldest son of a local farmer, was in a class of his own here – and the minister circulated his flock, telling stories of just marginal impropriety to suit the celebration, as the smoking, shouting, laughing, stone-throwing, eating, drinking, joking chapel let down its Baptist hair.

For the children, the beach was an Aladdin's cave of rock pools, sharpened breastbones of gannets (so perfectly denuded by the tide they were almost artefacts), planks of wood bearing ship-builders' skills, bleached boots hard as coconuts, glass balls, boxes, cork fenders, ropes, the skeletons of horses with flowing seaweed manes. Then they ran up the sky-path to the Muntan promontory where the high banks shut out the sea's roar, squeezed through the gateway where the same gate had hung drunkenly on one hinge for a score of years, into the field of black oats, ripening slowly in the salty air, belly-wriggling into the crop to gossip and tell stories, chewing the milky dough of the unripened grain, dimly conscious of the flying clouds through the rustling curtains of Black Tartary – the dusky oat variety grown near the sea.

Old Mr Pugh ate and drank with the best of them, which was just as well, because he made the next tea-party sadly memorable by falling on the pebbles and breaking his ancient thigh. He was carried out on a field gate, moaning less about the pain in his leg than the increasing liberties taken by wind and tide and the disappearance of the road across the pebbles. Eventually he died of pneumonia and his frail body was consigned on a day of sun and wind to the Llangloffan cemetery to the strains of a hymn written by the hymnologist of Abermawr, the great beach of God's sun and storm which, as with the road once used for the lime, got old Mr Pugh the Temperance fighter as well in the end.

The entry in Schoolin's Log for 16 May 1923, when school was closed for the 'Llangloffan Baptist Preaching Service', marked a very special day. The numerous figures in black bowlers and bonnets, in traps, on horseback, bicycles and on foot were on their way to the big chapel an hour earlier than customary, for the visiting preacher of the day – the Reverend Phillip Young – had experienced the fire of religious renewal which swept the Welsh industrial valleys just over twenty years before, when the Holy Spirit speaking through the mouth of Evan Roberts, the young Welsh miner, had seemed about to bring spiritual rebirth and redemption to the whole of Wales.

William Davis had installed a padded bench seat across his trap, with a chair, facing backwards, tied on behind. At half past nine he drew up outside his fellow deacon's cottage from which John John's wife, Bet, now emerged. She was shawled, short and round as though she were wearing a bustle, a long black skirt falling on to her still surprisingly neat small feet, and wearing an aged black Tam o'Shanter. Bet seldom went out, except to the chapel a few paces away, but she had attended those Evan Roberts meetings when convalescing after a long illness with her sister in the Mumbles, and was determined, despite her rheumatism, to attend Llangloffan to hear the good news just once more.

'Good morning, Bet fach, how lovely you are able to come.' Mr Davis touched his trilby, while John placed the specially built steps for Bet to climb painfully into the trap. Mr Davis held down the shafts until she was in her seat. Then, with John sitting behind, holding the little step ladder for use the other end, they drove slowly down the village street into a countryside where the husbandry of farming was still a silent skill and, apart from the barks of dogs and occasional words of command to the horses, the loudest sounds were from the lambs and the birds.

Bet was armed as far forward as possible into the already filling chapel, where men and women sat blamelessly apart, and where the deacons were already setting chairs under the trees outside for the overflow.

As far as her huge dewlap would allow her to turn her neck, Bet looked around the chapel where she had once been such a faithful member. Nothing had changed. The pews were clean and shiny, and the tribute plaques to William Lewis the hymnologist, glowed in the moted sunbeams. The pulpit still dominated the eye. She fumbled with her black leather hymn book, but the pages were a blur and John was not there to get the glasses from her skirt pocket. He was already in the Big Seat.

Now the chapel was full to overflowing and the Reverend Gilbert – the much loved, soon to be mourned but never forgotten pastor – came slowly down the aisle with the Reverend Phillip Young, one of the great preachers of Wales, tall, white-haired and with the handsome lined face of an actor, by his side. The first hymn was announced. They would begin with the true battle hymn of the Evan Roberts Revival – 'Thou art the all-forgiving God'. Bass and tenor, soprano and alto waited for the organ to play the introduction and then, at the lift of the precentor's hand, a sound as majestic as the Abermawr tide washed the chapel walls, beat against the oak roof, flowed through the open door and silenced the birds in the nearby elms. As feeling overflowed, the last verse was sung five times.

After prayers, more hymns and scripture readings, the Reverend Phillip then mounted the stairs to the pulpit in an atmosphere of rising exaltation. He began quietly, with just the occasional word of his welcome carrying promise of the great musical delivery to come, but within minutes, as he took the congregation with him to the Welsh valleys of the Revival, the preacher's *hwyl* began. His beautiful baritone voice planed and soared in a half-said half-sung recitative of rhythmical phrases, the thick lock of hair fell over his brow, and the arms eloquent now lifted in unison like the wings of an eagle, as though to bless.

He told his listeners of the confessions and repentance of sinners, and the miracles of rebirth and renewal he had personally witnessed, rousing John John and the other deacons to tempests of endorsing Amens and Allelulas in the Big Seat. He described how he had descended a coal-pit in the Rhondda to be present at a service in the pit-pony stables, how he had listened to a miner reading a passage from Matthew 6 to his mates, thrilled to the sound of the Revivalist hymns rolling through the underground galleries, where the shifts were dedicated to God. He told them how railway workers labelled carriages with legends that forbade cursing, how football matches changed to prayer meetings, and political gatherings to meetings of witness, how politicians were transformed into revivalists, and magistrates had reported being virtually unemployed.

And then he described the quartet of musical spinsters who were part of the Evan Roberts retinue. Bet, whose old heart was beating too fast and who had to sit down for all the hymns but whose eyes were shining, suddenly flew away, back to the promised land, to the little town of Gorseinion, near Swansea. There, twenty years ago, she had sat by Miss Priscilla Watkins in that famous meeting where Evan Roberts had fallen and remained prostrate and sobbing on the platform for ten minutes, to rise triumphant and radiant after being with Christ at Gethsemane and where Priscilla had suddenly risen in the congregation and electrified the meeting with her solo rendering of 'Here's my Bible, Dearest Jesus' to the tune of the 'Last Rose of Summer'. And Bet remembered how she too had felt an almost unbearable urge to join these witnessing ladies who went with Evan Roberts to all the meetings and soloed spontaneously from among the congregations and helped to bring 80,000 new converts to the Baptist fold. But for John, at home in St Nicholas, she too would have stayed.

The Reverend Phillip occupied the Llangloffan pulpit for one-and-a-half hours and after his great climactic ending, in which he denounced the sin of the times and called on Wales once again to lead the whole nation in prayer, the last verse of the last hymn was sung ten times and men and women came away purged and exalted.

Bet sat on until the chapel was nearly empty, and then John's strong arm helped her from her seat and slowly walked her to the door. William Davis was talking to the Reverend Phillip, whose hand was on his shoulder in a gesture of affection. Stiff and aching from her hours in the pew, Bet took a long time to climb into her seat in the trap. After the first burst of praise, the trio spoke little on the way home, for William was sunk deep in memory of the happy day when the Reverend Phillip had married him and his dear missus and that terrible day, over a quarter of a century ago, when she had died with his baby in childbirth.

Three Baptist juveniles – Tusks, Clogs and Voices – rode away from Llangloffan chapel, fiercely determined to become Baptist ministers themselves, a resolution which lasted for at least half of the panting, cycling miles of the uphill journey home.

CHAPTER SIX

Truth Among the Peardrops

'It was unanimously carried that the parish meeting authorise the Chairman and Clerk to sign an agreement on its behalf to have a telephone installed at St Nicholas Post Office.'

Meeting of the Parochial Electors of St Nicholas Parish, 6 September 1926

Arthur Bilbow, the grocer and postmaster, was a stooping stubbly-chinned Englishman who had married the previous tenant's daughter. Six feet two inches tall, with coarse vertical grey hair, a Woodbine always waggling from his lower lip, he supplied the necessities of life, both edible and inedible, and bought all the rabbits and most of the eggs and butter from the farms around. The unofficial division of labour between Bilbow and his wife Aggie – a plain, five foot tall, hook-nosed lady, with short-bobbed lank hair, and a regular shaver – was that Bilbow ran the shop, post office and trading connections, while she looked after the smallholding. Their nephew Jack helped with both.

The immediate impact of the shop was memorable, especially on the nose, for what one noticed first was the smell – or rather the smells, for the singular has a rather doubtful sound, and there was nothing unpleasant about the nose-cocktail one drank in Bilbow's store. Relative strength of the ingredients varied according to one's position. By the counter one absorbed the smell of flaky yeast sold from an open hessian bag, for beer-balm or baking. This mingled and competed, with diminishing success as the days passed, with the box of brown and gold bloaters, and the piled strings bought from the Breton, Johnny Onions. Further back, the shop gave out the smell of oranges, bulk prunes, currants, sultanas, sticky wedges of date, cheese, ground coffee, the cool fragrance of tea in foil-lined plywood chests. Everything except for oranges, eggs and chocolate was weighed by the grocer on counter scales equipped with little piles of brass weights. Right at the back where Bilbow operated as village postmaster and steamed open any letter that caught his fancy, the smell was of hot sealing wax, musty paper, paraffin, methylated spirits, carbolic soap, oil-skin coats and corduroy trousers, linseed oil and paint. If the door into the adjacent annexe was open, the nasal fare was enriched by fish meal, ground barley, spice and the smell of dead rabbits, rich, even exciting but sometimes dubious.

Inhaling the orange emanations as Schoolin entered for a packet of Shag, was William Evans, a village smallholder who worked a few acres with the help of his mother. He was much tormented by stomach pains though this had nothing to do with his job as a biting pig castrator who turned tiny boar pigs into hogs with his teeth (of which he had a wonderfully powerful set), usually before an admiring audience of juveniles.

He had this morning voiced disagreement on 'practical grounds' to Bilbow's plan for establishing a national racecourse 'behind the shop' – it was always '*behind*' the shop – and the shopkeeper was regarding him with the pitying smile, reserved for those who failed to share his visions.

'Ah, Evans,' he remonstrated, shaking his head in sorrow at such ignorance, 'practical you say, is it practical? All right, let me ask you in turn, what do you mean by practical?'

'Is the ether practical? Is a mollecewle practical? Is a newborn baby practical? Hey? Have you read the *Science of Life* by Wells and Huxley? No, I thought you hadn't, Mr Evans, I thought you hadn't . . .'

The parish castrator fled in relief as Schoolin advanced to the counter.

'Ah, Mr Jones,' the shopkeeper began and he leaned back in the shadows to support his long back, 'I'm glad you've called. I've been meaning to have a word with you for some time. . . .'

Knowing from experience that he could end up in a web mumbo-jumbo, Schoolin broke in hastily, 'Some other time, Bilbow, some other time. My wife is wanting some potatoes from the garden. Just a packet of Shag, please.'

Bilbow opened the counter flap and with a firm 'This won't take a minute, Mr Jones, not a minute . . .' half-cajoled, half-pulled Schoolin into a room where chairs were piled high with books, with sauce bottles and meal debris still on the table. He cleared a space, waved Schoolin down, lit a Woodbine, and pressed one on his guest.

'I want to have a word with you about this,' he said. 'It's a book I have just received from Haverfordwest County Library. Tell me now, what do you think about this?' and opening the large Rabelais tome he began to read in solemn tones putting the spoken emphasis in the middle syllable of each name. *The Most Fearful Life of the Great Gargantewa, Father of Pantagrewel, composed many years ago by Master Alcobribas, Abstractor of the Quinty Sense.* He looked up, with an expression of triumph. 'You know, Mr Jones, I believe this book – and I may say it has taken Mr Dickman the Librarian a long time to get it at all – has got *all the answers to the secrets of the universe* . . .' He punctuated the words with a forefinger.

Already beginning to enjoy, despite himself, the inspired lunacy of the shopkeeper, Schoolin decided he must escape, but before he could do more than half rise from the chair, was waved down again and introduced to two other tomes, *The Tibetan Book of the Dead* and *The Secrets of the Kabalah*, recently arrived through the post. Fifteen minutes elapsed before he was able to possess his tobacco and escape from the world of Gargantua into his garden.

Schoolin, who got to know the Haverfordwest Librarian at a later date, found a bureaucrat mystified by the literary demands of the St Nicholas grocer, which he had to scour libraries all over Wales to satisfy.

Nobody could really understand Bilbow or be certain whether his weird pursuits and his tirades of mumbo-jumbo were a game to mystify, not to say awe, those around him, or whether in some dimly felt fashion he believed the rubbish he talked. It is doubtful whether he made any sustained attempt to read the volumes delivered by post to the shop. Otherwise, a literal interpretation of Rabelais must certainly have strained even Bilbow's credulity. Who knows and what matter anyhow? For, what dividends he doled his customers, this zany village grocer, crouched like a seedy wizard in the gloaming of his store, bombarding rabbit trappers and roadmen and farmers, schoolmaster, rector and anybody else who failed to escape in time, with his weird philosophical allsorts.

For Schoolin's son, it was a piece of special good fortune that the St Nicholas grocer should have formed a high opinion of his listening power.

'Ah, Lawellin,' he would say as Llewelyn came into the shop 'just for a little chat' with his mind on peardrops, 'sit down by here and put your feet by there, boy. Always let the blood flow to your brains, Lawellin.'

If goodies were a little slow in arriving, Llewelyn learned that by affecting to rise with the statement that he 'had to go home now', the grocer would invariably reply, 'No, no, Lawellin, my dear, I'm sure you don't have to go. I'm enjoying this, you know. Here, would you like a fig?' Or it might be 'a tube of sherbet', and splendid hours were spent, chewing, munching, sucking, as the tirades of high falutin' fiddlesticks flowed past his ears.

As one learned in ether, ectoplasm, reincarnation and Gargantua, the grocer was in the van of all scientific progress and, as a friend of Marconi, the natural transmitter of the miracle of wireless to St Nicholas. Yet much to Bilbow's (and Aggie's) annoyance, the

first wireless appeared in the Squire's drawing-room. Schoolin and his wife and Llewelyn were among those invited across, to be greeted at the front door by the Squire's tall, stately lady, with the words, 'Come in, it's on, it's music, you know.'

The Squire was hosting a military march, white Van Dyck beard and auctioneer's hand acknowledging the beat as though accepting bids. Accustomed to lording it from the rostrum, he was a true autocrat in retirement. He walked through the village with a limp and stick, his stern gaze missing nothing. He imposed a uniformity on his tenants which denied their right to a scintilla of individuality where his property was concerned. Schoolin's insistence on surrounding the white of his windows with a thin line of blue – 'like a picture in a frame' – produced a thunder of denunciation from the passing tyrant which could be heard from the village shop eighty yards away.

But the Squire's expression when his visitors were ushered into his drawing-room was benevolent as he dispensed the largesse of wireless to the upper members of his tenantry. Then the music ended and the announcer began to speak in the sort of indistinct tone which is unacceptable to any self-respecting auctioneer. Mr James rose to twiddle the knobs. The voice was immediately swallowed in the din of a thousand cricket balls landing on Schoolin's nearby zinc-roofed shed. Squire turned the knob again, confidently at first, but then with increasing desperation until, choleric and accusing, he shouted for Daniel Evans his chauffeur-cum-handyman, who was standing outside the window. 'Evans, come here' but though Daniel entered with servile alacrity and began to twiddle, the racket worsened. The Squire shouted, 'Turn it off, Evans, turn the damn thing off, damn you, you obviously don't know anything about it, man.'

Nor could the set be made to work again until expert help was brought from Fishguard.

News of thé fiasco was received by Bilbow with glee, and he explained at length to his customers that the set was far too weak for the St Nicholas ether, that Sir Oliver Lodge had told him there was a need for a minimum eight valves, and that the custom-built monster was already en route to his shop.

When the set arrived, with a forest of knobs and a bulbous piece of glass like a squid's eye, Bilbow announced a concert in the village school, employed the grave digger to dig a hole for the fir pole aerial which soared higher than the school belfry, and the machine was transported with caution to the school by horse and trap.

The schoolroom was packed when Bilbow rose to an ovation, though some of the clapping was from the bloods at the back, which was not a dependable form of witness. Flashing grey dentures, he addressed the meeting.

'People of St Nicholas, welcome to my Concert. Tonight we are putting St Nicholas on the map. I have made arrangements for

programmes from Hilversum and the Eiffel Tower and of course from 2LO. My wireless has been specially built with eight powerful valves because the St Nicholas ether is not strong enough for only four. As you know, the four-valve system has already been tried. But I don't need to tell you about that. He! He! Ho! Ho! And I am planning later on to have a transmitter as well as a receiver for our village. Then people as far as India will be able to hear the wonderful singing in Llangloffan chapel. And now, ladies and gentlemen, I know you are waiting impatiently and don't want to wait any longer and so I bid you welcome to – Radio St Nicholas' – he finished with a flourish.

He stooped to the set, switched on, stood upright and explained it needed time to warm. Then with a suddenness which made the shopkeeper and the assembly jump, the Flying Scotsman hauling a hundred trucks of loose zinc sheets arrived through the speaker, announcing its arrival with continuous screeching blasts.
Bilbow turned down the volume.

'Give it some home-brewed, Bilbow,' shouted a voice from the back.

Bilbow restored the volume and the audience now heard the yowling of all the tomcats in Wales in frenzied choir. He switched off. He tried again and again and the mood of expectancy began to dim until, suddenly discernible behind the din, there came the sound of voices singing 'Silent Night' in harmony. It was sung right through, followed by frenzied clapping and stamping and loud requests for encores. Then as the Flying Scotsman threatened to return, Bilbow turned down the volume. In the silence a mysterious 'Cock a Doodle Doo' was heard, followed by the words 'Bum to Bilbow' and with the realisation that four bloods from the back, led by Telyn Lamb who sang with the plangency of the harp after which he was named, had gone out to sing under the window, the audience began to rock and jeer and giggle. The angry grocer came charging from the platform with the words 'Out of my way, I'll show the buggers' and disappeared outside, chasing his quarry unsuccessfully through the dark village street while in the front row seat of honour poor Mrs Bilbow waited, with a neck engulfed in a tide of scarlet.

Bilbow never caught the singers nor, after more trying, did he capture the 2LO voices in the ether that night, and the audience had recourse instead to a more dependable form of entertainment. The piano was manhandled to the front, a mixed choir flowered, and sang 'Myfanwy' and other old favourites with Llewelyn's mother accompanying. This was followed by a bald entertainer from the Pen Caer coast who sang three breast and bottom 'comic' songs, a dramatic Welsh recitation about 'The Old Clock', and 'The Roast Beef of Old England' by a farmyard baritone. The village had risen to the occasion from the ashes of Bilbow's failure.

The following day when Llewelyn visited the shop, the grocer looked pensive and grey. He placed a hand on his chest and shook his head sorrowfully before bringing up a huge belch with the words, 'I don't feel at all well today, Lawellin bach. I've got nasty old wind round the heart, really nasty old wind.'

There was no mention of 2LO, or Sir Oliver Lodge, or Marconi or any other of his treacherous friends.

The installation of the telephone in the Post Office part of the shop enhanced Bilbow's status, and its occasional use by those brave enough – the instrument provoked something near terror among the older inhabitants – was invested with a grace-and-favour policy by the grocer, which was a source of annoyance to those who used it to make calls. Bilbow's proprietorial attitude so incensed Schoolin's wife, Catherine, on one occasion when she was told by Aggie she would have to wait a long time 'because Mr Bilbow is on the wire on important Government business' that she expressed her opinion that most of the 'on the wire business' was fictitious and that there was nobody at the other end of the line. Bilbow certainly appeared to spend long intervals with the receiver glued to his ear, and many a customer entered to a raised hand enjoining silence as the grocer received his real or mythical tidings over the wire.

The telephone installation, however, was delayed by juvenile initiative for two weeks. On the Thursday evening, Gwilym Thomas – the stone-throwing hero of those chapel beach tea-parties – skidded his bike to a stop in front of the shop, called over a quartet of smaller children which included Llewelyn and Tusks and, cupping his mouth furtively, said in a stage whisper, 'Let's go smash some bloody pots, shall us, eh? Come on, I'll show yer . . .'

Today, the power and prowess of Gwilym's left arm would have earned him fame with javelin or discus. But the only missiles in St Nicholas were stones, and five minutes after pedalling furiously out of the village, Gwilym and his acolytes were dismounting near long, rectangular barrows of stone prepared for road-mending.

'Here, get us some stones and mind you pick the right 'uns then,' Gwilym said. He held up a sample which he hefted lovingly in his big left hand. 'Not too big, not too small, like this 'un.' A few minutes later, pockets bulging and weighing down their trousers, they followed him towards the nearest pole without wires but with china insulators shining on the crosspiece.

Gwilym stopped, looked round, moved a few yards out to widen the angle and with a hoarse, 'Now watch that bloody pot go flyin'', sent the first stone whistling past the pole.

'Missed, by damn' he said disgustedly. He took another stone in his left hand, lifted his arm and this time stayed motionless a moment as though willing the path to the pot. The stone hit it dead-centre with a sound like the crack of Jockey-Joe the horse-breaker's whip. The pieces falling into the road brought the ammunition carriers to the verge of panic until Gwilym arrested them with a lifted stone. They stayed and palpitatingly doled out the thunderbolts and, as the tally mounted and fear vanished, they began to enjoy themselves and share the power of the rural Jove. Then, with the mayhem over, they stole back to the crossroads and, knit together by shared excitement, returned to their bikes. But before departing, Gwilym listed blood-curdling punishments he would deal out to anyone who breathed a word, especially to Tusks, the youngest and least dependable, for whom he outlined a peculiarly unpleasant stomach-removing operation.

The following morning Llewelyn woke, wide-eyed with apprehension, to find a frightened Tusks already outside.

'There's a hobble we're in,' he wailed. 'They'll take us to Mathry and put us in jail . . .'

The Mathry bobby's arrival at school at 11.30 a.m. made the crime official.

'Stand up,' Schoolin shouted to the Big Room when he received the news of the ten broken insulators from P.C. Price.

His angry eyes probed the faces in front of him and, mindful of the deadly left arm which dominated the school rounders sessions, he pointed and barked, 'What do you know about this, Gwilym Thomas? Where were you last night then, eh?'

Gwilym stood to attention. 'Please sir, I was helping my mother in the garden. My mother wanted the potatoes lifting.'

It was a cunning alibi, calculated to turn away wrath. Gwilym's father had taken to his bed ten years before, with melancholia. Even before that, he had for years sat in the inglenook dolefully milking the deathwish while his bowed little wife sat in the byre and milked the cows, earning the sympathy of the parish as she

94

fought gallantly to bring up their three children. Gwilym was the eldest, and his mother's right hand.

So Schoolin's gaze wavered and moved on, the conspiracy held firm, the bobby departed with dudgeon but no culprit, and two weeks later Bilbow was officially installed on the wire.

Perhaps, unconsciously, Gwilym had been taking revenge against a fate about to deal the family a cruel blow, for a month after the pot-smashing, the bailiffs moved in. On the day of the forced sale, the equipment was piled in little lots, much of it hardly more than junk. Gwilym had polished the ploughshare, put black paint on the body, burnished the harrow teeth with a file, smartened up the farm cart, waggon and wheelbarrow with orange paint, but the stock told the story. The three farm horses, thin, languid and spiritless, resting with tilted hooves, waited for buyer or knacker; the eight cows, pin bones like hat stands, unmilked since the previous night to try and gorge their udders to respectable size, slowly leaked milk on to the hard-packed earthen floor of the byre, and were worth very little of anyone's money.

Walking round the back of the house, Llewelyn found Gwilym, his tearful face buried in the neck of the farm collie, and stole away. The takings were pitiable as was the appearance of the father, dressed in overcoat and best black suit, face white as the muffler round his wasted throat, eyes sick and reproachful, half-led half-carried to the car which took him away. The farm remained derelict and empty for a long time until an unexpected new tenant was found from the village.

Whenever Bilbow's wife Aggie became too disillusioned with the drudgery of her lot, and her soiled towel began to flash round

his ears with painful frequency, there was one very, very special dream to which he had recourse, to cool her down. This was the prospective purchase of a *real farm* with many more acres than the muddy smallholding that went with the shop. This was always Aggie's golden dream.

The funds which were to place her and Arthur in their broad acres were in prospect from an unusual source. Arthur claimed first cousin relationship with William Willet, the West London originator of daylight saving, who was always referred to by Aggie as the 'old gentleman'. Bilbow claimed that William Willet's brainwave should be subject to royalties, payable to members of the family 'just like the royalties from a quarry'. The prospect of this largesse never failed to waft poor Aggie out of her laborious time-and-place into her dreamland.

Alas, realisation came not from the crock of gold at the foot of Bilbow's daylight-saving rainbow for, as time went on, his rabbit and animal feed business began to fade and the increasing mobility of the village took more and more people into nearby Fishguard to shop. So he and Aggie decided to take the tenancy of the farm left by Gwilym's family, where they pottered on from crisis to crisis. And such is the fecklessness of memory that the man who for years had dominated the trade in the parish and been a household word for his eccentricities, was quickly drowned in the sea of time.

It was at the farm, years later, that a grown-up Llewelyn on leave from Dunkirk went to look for his old friend. He knocked at the door of the ram-shackle farmhouse and after a lengthy silence, watched the door drag open and the collarless figure appear, smoking the inevitable Woodbine, the stubble now almost white, but the vertical shock of hair still profuse and wiry.

He had an anxious expression for he was not accustomed to opening the door to friends but mostly to creditors at that time. After a moment's puzzled frown, memory returned, his face brightened and he flashed a smile of recognition and pleasure.

'Lawellin, Lawellin,' he said and reached forward with both hands. Then he turned round and called with eagerness, 'Aggie, Aggie, you'll never guess who it is. It's Lawellin, Lawellin Jones.'

For what seemed a long time, there was no reply from the dark interior and then a small reedy voice was heard calling, 'Well, ask him in then, Bilbow, ask him in.'

Arthur moved forward a pace and partially closed the door, bent his head and said, 'The Missus hasn't been very well lately, Llawellin bach. But don't say anything.' He put a finger to his lips to enjoin silence.

Inside the room was gloomy, for the curtains were drawn and as his eyes became accustomed, Llewelyn saw a figure huddled over a paraffin stove in the inglenook, a gnome with a face hardly more than the size of a human heart in which the white features of Aggie were discernible.

Bilbow waved him forward with the words, 'Here's Lawellin, Aggie. Come in and sit down, Lawellin bach.'

Aggie stirred a welcoming hand on her lap and Llewelyn moved forward to take it in his own. It was nerveless and cold.

'Hello, Mrs Bilbow,' he said softly, 'how nice to see you after all this time. And how are you?' He realised he was whispering.

Her voice, like her face and her hand, was shrunken, bearing no relation to the towel-flashing Aggie of former days. But she clenched her hand and said with a touch of the old determination, speaking slowly and with difficulty, 'I've not been very well. But I've promised Bilbow I'll be up and about for the haymaking, and Dr Ewen has given me some new pills. Did you know we're running the farm ourselves? Jack left us, you see. But I'm sure I'll be all right for the haymaking.'

There was a long pause as she gathered strength, to continue. 'Did you notice how the grass is growing? Bilbow says it's one of the earliest springs for years. That's a godsend for us. We've been very short of hay, you know.'

Llewelyn looked at Bilbow, gentle-faced, grey and elderly now, playing a silent listening role. Then suddenly there came a flash of the old flatterer, and he looked across at his wife.

D

'You *must* come and see us when we're making hay, Lawellin, it's Aggie making rick and me pitching. Aggie is a champion rick-maker.'

Aggie smiled at the tribute but didn't say any more until Llewelyn bade her a gentle goodbye, when she rallied and told him mind to come back in July for the haymaking and, as though she had to pay tribute to the days which he had spent with Jack and Puss – the mare who used to pull the trap on the rabbit-collecting journeys – said with painful slowness, 'It's a pity Bilbow couldn't have kept the rabbits. The income would have been very useful. You and Jack had good times in those days.'

Bilbow accompanied him outside and as they shook hands, he said, 'It's her back passage, Lawellin,' and lifted his hands in dismay.

Llewelyn mounted his bike and rode mistily past fields, where the harbingers of that early spring held no good news for Aggie, nor the pitifully thin cattle which, after winter starvation, were killed by the high protein herbage.

After Aggie's death, the remaining farm possessions were sold and Bilbow was last seen by a farm worker one morning in May carrying a suitcase, hurrying with long stride and bowed head towards the railway station. He never appeared in the area again.

But that is not how he is remembered by Llewelyn, going away in defeat, but as the King Arthur of his zany village prime, dishing out the peardrops to the small boy who sat sucking noisily among the oodles and lashings of the grocer's Goshen, listening to *The Secrets of the Kabalah* and the *Tibetan Book of the Dead* and the secrets and glories of other vanished kingdoms.

CHAPTER SEVEN

Taste of Spring

'St David's Day. Every child in the School wore a daffodil . . .'
Headmaster's Log Book, 1 March 1926

Spring came to school with flowers and lambs. The flowers came
long before the lambs, for there was hardly a period when the
earthen-heated parish banks were not somewhere in bloom.
Indeed it was observation during the nineteen thirties of the early
flowering of hedgerow plants – as early as the Scilly Isles – which
led to the establishment of the Pembrokeshire early potato industry
which was to prove a lifeline for the parish farmers.

January started with white sweet-smelling handfuls of escapee
snowdrops, cartloads of cream primroses in February, and by
St David's day, daffodils, half bud, half flower, fluttered gold and
green flags in the breezy fields of the manor house near
Abermawr. Each year the village children climbed into the daffodil
fields, tearing at the clumps like young stirks in spring clover, in
fear that the bailiff who carried a whip might catch them picking or
tying loads to bicycle carriers that laid golden trails to the village.

Spring arrived to the music of hedgerow whistles. First efforts began at the end of March when buds of hedge sycamore were pushing out pale green spikes, tinged with pink, covered with pale silky hairs, though best results came later when both the tinted veined leaves as well as flowers were fully formed.

Then the shoots, thick as walking sticks, were cut off and trimmed into six-inch lengths, scored round with a penknife an inch from the end. The sugary wand was soaked with spittle, and then, holding it rigid in a handkerchief, first attempts made to loosen the bark. It had to come off – snickingly – in one piece or one had to begin again. Then with a little channel to let in air, and the bark replaced and pulled over the tapering mouthpiece, the whistle was ready to join the birds – though unlike those music-makers, sycamore whistles became gurgley with spit. Llewelyn also made a special whistle from two of his father's brass cartridge tops which, with the centres removed, produced much-envied notes and provided a cold, brassy taste when they lay in the mouth.

Whistles were drowned by rowdier notes when hooping began. All winter, they had lain forgotten in outhouses and yards, but when April arrived, they were winkled out and the hooping season was ready to begin.

'Come on,' yelled Collars Morgan, 'last to follow gets 'is 'ead chopped off,' and set off towards the smithy, with the rusty hoops complaining like a crop of capons. But the screech soon vanished, and old skills revived, until by the downhill approach to school, the hoops were running as sweet as foxes. Then Collars Morgan gave a mighty swipe to his hoop which, invested with a wayward devil, jumped through the bottom window pane and came to rest against Schoolin's desk. As Collars had daubed it with a white 'M-O-R-G-A-N' there was no need for Schoolin to seek the offender on Monday morning and after school had finished its breathless 'We are but little children meek . . .', Collars was called

forth to receive two hard thwacks on each hand, the hands being
reserved for offences of gravity.

After the first day, hoops were supplemented with Old Bandin,
the iron tyre off a trap wheel, belaboured down the village street
with a broom handle so that as it passed the shop, the waiting
experts sent their hoops at right angles – hopefully – through the
iron rim. A notable success was scored one evening by Tusks who
sent his circlet through the wobbling circumference but at the
wrong point, for it careered through the partly opened door of the
chapel, ran silently down the carpeted aisle and climbed up the
back of John John, the praying trapper. He thought he was being
attacked by the Evil One himself, whom at that moment he was
blaming for the record number of affiliation orders and paternity
cases in the parish, which had followed on the rising sap of the
previous spring.

Children in St Nicholas, school and holiday time alike, literally
smelled of spring and summer from bruising and pulling, picking
and squeezing the scents and saps of stalks and roots and leaves
and flowers, inhaling like snuff addicts their attars and essences.
But while there was plenty with which to fill the nose, there was
hardly anything to chew. So the prospect of a source of free
victuals for the Easter holidays, suggested by Collars Morgan, was
a winner when he produced the idea in the playground on the last
day of term.

He was surrounded by minions, dutifully oohing and aahing his
skills as a propellor of spit. After a shot which landed on target
eight feet away, he swallowed the rest of his ammunition and said,
'Do ye know wot, you buggers, d'ye know wot? I knows about some
plovers' heggs. I'll let you buggers 'ave a feed if yer like . . .'

Feed. The magic word fell like a ripe apple among the listeners who never seemed to have enough to eat anyhow, especially those who walked miles to school and began to raid their dinner bags almost within sight of home.

But the proposition was not clear, so Clogs Evans, seldom without a bun or a piece of bread and whose jaws were the nearest thing to perpetual motion in the village, asked eagerly, 'Feed? Wot feed then, Collars? Wotcha mean?'

Gold-stud Collars shifted his eyes fractionally in Clogs' direction, for he hardly rated direct address.

'Feed of heggs boiled in a saucepan in Abermawr.'

This prospect of orgy was too much for Clogs, for he began to jump up and down with gasping, yumming sounds.

Then little Tusks piped up in breathless falsetto, 'Why don't we 'ave maggypies too then, Collars?'

The group waited for Collars to wipe the presumptuous Tusks and his maggypies off the playground but instead he gave him an approving smile and replied, 'Yeah', and then in a rising tone as full implications flooded in, 'Yeah, good idea, Tusks boy. We could 'ave linnets too . . .'

As though Collars had commanded the withdrawal of a communal finger from some sort of ornithological dyke, the names of all the birds that could be thought of flew back and forth in the playground until the glowing Tusks, made incautious by success, piped again, 'How about wrens then, Collars?'

At this, he was replaced in the peck order with a contemptuous, 'Wrens is too bloody small, like you, you blooming daft twit. Why don't you be yer age and shrrup?'

With the rest of the gang nodding approval, they went into class.

The egg gang reassembled briefly after school when, to the original Collars, Croakers (Collar's younger brother, who was passing through a prolonged voice-breaking phase), Clogs, Tusks, Llewelyn, were added Voices, whose father was a choir conductor, and the son of the oily genius who travelled the steam threshing outfit round the farms, who was nicknamed Dragon after the title on his father's steamer.

The following morning, Llewelyn and Tusks went rummaging and burrowing, finding and looting purple and white eggs from a tiny ditchside nest of grass, moss- and hair-lined; greenish-blue eggs from a mossy cup in a tracery of twigs; a bonanza of ten brown pheasant eggs from a nest totally hidden by leaves and twigs but given away by the last minute eruption of the brooding bird –

an act that would really have had Schoolin breaking his cane on their bottoms – and finally, seven unattended mallard eggs by the pond of Lloyd's Field near the village. Llewelyn took them home and hid them in the coalhouse.

At half past nine on Easter Monday all the group except Voices had made their way to Abermawr and with hair in golliwog disarray, were standing round Collars in a semi-circle. An aged iron saucepan lay at his feet.

The leader appeared to be in no hurry to begin, so that the ever-hungry Clogs, appetite whetted by the sea breezes, was constrained to break rank with a plaintive question.

'When we going to start the Feed then, Collars?'

He took half a grey scruffy-looking bun from his pocket, pushed most of it into his mouth in one go, and champing like a horse said in muffled tones, 'I got a hawful 'ungriness. I had my breakfast more than a hower ago.'

Collars did not favour Clogs with a direct glance but turning slightly west-by-north so the breeze was behind him, ejected a gout of spit through his teeth which landed ten feet away.

Then he said to Clogs, 'Alwright then, you start. You'm the 'ungriest. Where's your heggs then.'

Clogs brought out a paper bag from his pocket from which he took a small brown egg, and then a huge white one.

'A bantam and a *goose*,' he said proudly. 'I stole 'em,' he added, half-closing both his little eyes simultaneously in what was meant to be a wink.

Collars was unimpressed and pointing to the sand at his feet said, 'They aint wild 'uns, is they, you twit, but put 'em down by there.'

He turned to the next member. 'Wotcha got then, Dragon,' he asked and the group gaze fell on the peaky-faced boy with china-blue eyes.

'Divers' eggs,' he said, 'two each. I got 'em on Castell Mawr.'

'Bloomin' good, Dragon, very bloomin' good, very good heggs. Put 'em by there,' and Collars reached across to shake the intrepid Dragon by the hand – for Castell Mawr, the Iron Age fortress rock, had a very difficult approach above a seal-haunted creek. The rest of the company nodded their endorsement.

Then it was the turn of Llewelyn whose pseudonym was Skin and Bones.

'Let's 'ave a look at your heggs then, Skin,' said the Leader.

Llewelyn laid the offerings one by one on the sand at the

leader's feet, and earned immediate approval.

'Very good work, Skin boy, very good heggs,' said Collars.

He reached forward, lifted and hefted one of the small blue ones and glancing across said, 'The little 'uns is just right for Tusks.'

It was now the turn of Collars himself. First came eight plover eggs placed side by side on the sand, and he gave an accompanying commentary.

'Plovers,' he said, pronouncing it as in 'overs', and added the site of discovery, 'Trefasser Farm'.

Then came three large red and white eggs. Collars glanced round briefly and said, 'Boozeards. Garn Fawr.'

Then came seven white eggs to which Collars added the laconic comment, 'Goodhyoos. Pen-y-Groes.'

Next, with no allocation of site, a final six, in brown and grey livery, overlaid with a blueish tinge, allocated to 'Maggypies'.

Collars then began to allocate jobs.

'Clogs, you and Tusks go and get the blooming water.'

Clogs looked puzzled. 'Where'll I get the water then?' he asked.

Collars stared in unbelief. 'Where'd do you think you'll get it from, you daft twit. From the blooming sea, of course.'

'Schoolin's son, you and Croakers get the wood. Dragon'll give us a hand by 'ere with the fire.'

With responsibilities discharged, and the wood laid to satisfaction, Collars took a bottle from his pocket and, placing it near a few wisps of hay he had brought, explained it was 'blooming paraffin'. He looked round and struck a hand-cupped match which the wind blew out. He was successful with the next. The paraffined hay flared, the wood caught, tongues of breeze-fanned flame licked out, and quite soon the cauldron began to bubble and give off a smell like the Fishguard Gents' urinal.

Peering through the steam like some fledgling sorcerer cooking up spells, Collars announced his verdict that the eggs were ready. He told Dragon to 'get hold by 'ere' and jointly holding a piece of

wood, they lifted the bubbling crock off the fire and carried it to
the sea, to flood out the boiling water. They returned with the
crock and the great moment had arrived.

The gang leaned forward. Results were mixed. The goose egg
which dwarfed the collection had been overlaid with rufous haze
from the iron saucepan. The cormorant's eggs had a bluish tinge,
those of the bullfinch a dim green, and the buzzard eggs looked as
though some of the red had run. A few had succumbed to the heat
and were encircled with collars of grey round the cracks. There was
a crust of salt round the rim of the saucepan. The general effect
was unappetising. Even the insatiable Clogs, preparing to greet the
spectacle of largesse with a yumming sound, was left with his
mouth half open.

Collars looked round the group and chose Tusks to open the
orgy, tossing him the tiny blue egg which now looked more than
ever like a pebble.

''Ere Tusks boy,' he said, ''ere you, you'm the smallest, get
crackin'.'

Tusks eventually managed to peel off the shell. He had,
however, no front teeth, and either had to pop the unknown egg
into his mouth or explore it from the side. He chose the discreet
course, giving the company a ghastly smile with the thrush egg
impaled on his left canine. Collars scowled, shrugged his shoulders,
and lobbed over a plover's egg to each of the gang. They tapped
the still warm shell and bit into the strong but familiar taste of
egg, with relieved 'yums'.

Then the crunch of feet announced the belated arrival of Voices.
It was a woebegone rabbit-trapper's son who stood above the
group.

'I aint got no heggs, Collars. I had to help my Dad oil his traps. But I brought some blooming salt . . . ' he said, bringing out a tin marked Dark Rich Honeydew.

'Good boy, Voices, just wot we wanted. Pass it round, Voices,' said Collars and Voices circulated the group like a priest, dropping a pinch in each outstretched palm.

Collars now distributed a helping from the pheasant, a disappointing second course, with a strong smell and taste of rotten onions. There was a spitting out of first mouthfuls.

'Ugh a fi,' said Collars. 'We'll try the howl.' But the eggs of the night hunter were even worse, easily the least acceptable to date, with a strong acid flavour overlaid with carbolic.

To restore confidence with something more familiar, Collars passed round the duck eggs. But alas, the eggs of the mallard are not keepers and this lot was as thoroughly nasty as the buckets over which the village had sat for so long.

As though he could read the future, Clogs suddenly blurted, 'Wot about my goose hegg then, Collars. I'll 'ave my goose hegg now. Give it to me Collars.'

But ignoring Clogs, Collars rose with a vomiting sound and as spots of rain began to freckle the pebbles, started to fling the remaining maggypie, buzzard, yellow hammer, bullfinch, bantam and sparrow eggs into the Abermawr waves. Last to go with a mighty fling was the goose egg, despite Clog's cry of 'Not my goose one, Collars.'

The crock was empty and as the rain began to pour, Collars seized the empty vessel and ran from the beach, followed by the

others with Tusks falling increasingly behind. They reached the canopy of the trees on their bicycles as the rain began to sheet and, secure from the deluge, watched Tusks weaving and swerving as he stood on the pedals of his small bike. He arrived like a rag and bone gnome baptised in his clothes, fell off his bike, then rose and without warning threw up a combination of bread and jam and plover egg.

At this, Collars diagnosed in a solemn voice, 'Them heggs was too rich. He'll need senna pods.'

Then the rain stopped, the sky cleared, the banqueters rode to the fork where, with nods and winks and so-longs, they went their various ways. The Feed was over.

Despite his tribulations, it was Tusks who brought up the possibility of a future orgy at the beginning of the summer term.

'When we going to 'ave another Feed then, Collars?'

Collars looked at him pensively. 'Yeah, he said. 'Yeah. Good idea, Tusks boy.'

He indicated the field near the school with a jerk of his head. 'But I'll tell yer something, I'll tell yer something straight. We won't 'ave no more heggs. Drop dead, yer can't depend on heggs. Next time we'll have musharoons.' With the aid of gravity, he scored a spit bulleye on a frog in the marsh ten feet below just as Schoolin began to wave the handbell which summoned the school to the sung afternoon grace which would be bawled with equal enthusiasm by Churchgoers and Baptists alike.

CHAPTER EIGHT

The Logan Stone

'In this wild stony parish are several cromlechs.'
Archaeologia Cambrensis Vol V 5th Series, 1888

One fine blue afternoon when the parish of St Nicholas was bathed
in that hallowing North Pembrokeshire light which has enchanted
and challenged so many artists over the years – John Piper and
Graham Sutherland are modern exemplars – Collars Morgan led
his minions charging out of the sunlit village, mounted on forked
sticks. Their progress was irregular because of shying steeds and

because, from time to time, the leader halted and broke into a loud cry of 'every egg a bird', a raucous warranty which he had borrowed from the 'Fowlman' who sold hatching eggs at the weekly Fishguard market below the Town Hall clock.

The destination that afternoon was Trevayog Farm which nestles beneath the great wall of rock which forms the foam-girdled peninsula of Pen Caer. Entering the narrow Trevayog lane, they spied the farmer's son watching their approach from the top of a field bank. Collars got down immediately to the business in hand.

'Where's the bloomin' stone then, Gord,' he shouted.

From his high position, the farmer's son, a fair-haired boy of twelve with wild blue eyes and who attended school in the next parish, pointed past the black pine-end of the farmhouse. Then with a cry of 'Follow me as fast as yer can', he leapt down and with hobnailed boots clattering on the stony lane, led them towards the pellucid Trevayog farm pond, the cleanest and clearest and most beautiful of all ponds round about, and holding today in its shining depths the cloud-capped breasts of the nearby tumulus of Garn Fawr.

They reached the stony eminence of Garn Bica where their guide raised his hand, pointed and said, 'There she is by there. My father found her.'

The stone in question was shaped rather like a cromlech capstone and was half-buried in the greensward. Subject to formal approval by a committee seconded from the Parish Council, the stone had been put forward by the farmer as having the right shape and size to serve as the 'Logan', the Proclamation Stone from which the Archdruid of Wales, surrounded by white-robed fellow druids, would proclaim the opening of the National Eisteddfod, soon to be held at nearby Fishguard.

Collars, however, was determined not to be impressed and having used it as a target for a virtuoso spit, leapt the stone

lengthways and widthways with derisive ease, followed by his
leaping minions. Then Tusks, who was a poor jumper but who
needed minimal encouragement to open up at any time,
unbuttoned his trousers and dribbled a wavery personal signature
of water across the stone, an act which, in the later judgement of
Collars Morgan, had consequences which could only be described
as fantastic, if not unique.

When the news first broke that St Nicholas was to go for the
supreme honour of providing the Logan, the parish had been swept
with a blaze of gorse-fire enthusiasm, and it was less than forty-
eight hours before the news was brought to Schoolin that the
suitable stone had been found on Trevayog. The approval of the
Inspection Committee was a formality, for the farmer had selected
a beauty, and on the following day he dug round the half-buried
stone to facilitate winkling it out for the trolley – already delivered
to the village by Farmer Beynon of Trefelgarn Farm – which the
smith and the carpenter had strengthened with heavy planks from
the creek of Pwll Deri, three miles away, the richest source of
shipwreck timber along the coastline. Then the smith forged a
triangular tow-bar, fire-welding and boring one molten end into
an eye for the iron horse.

The steam engine came from nearby Mathry, dressed in its
Sunday best, title gleaming, brass trapping shining gold, buffer and
boiler plates bright as a robin's breast, black body agleam, and
then, hissing, clanking and whistle-blowing, with the trolley
trundling behind, it made the journey to the site where the
blacksmith took charge. Guiding the engine into line, he looped
the wire rope round the dug-out end of the seven-foot monster
stone which had been lying there since the Pleistocene Age, until
it was lifted upright, sitting on its bottom like a giant before
overbalancing on to the end of the trolley. But it fell faster than

planned – a faint crack appeared across the point of impact, but it had not gone deep and, to a chatter of relief, followed by a ragged cheer, the monolith was winched forward to its proper resting place.

By two o'clock on Saturday afternoon, the convoy, with every able-bodied male in the parish en cortège, was on its way to Fishguard. The turning into Ffynon Druidion farm, where the road passes through the yard, is a right-angled one and the driver made a wide sweep to bring his load neatly into line between the stone gateposts. And then the disaster occurred. The backwheel of the trolley rode over a stone in the road, came down with a chilling jar felt by everybody, and the giant stone parted at the point of the original crack as neatly as a halved apple.

Staring in awe and big-eyed astonishment, Collars Morgan called his four minions to his side and jerking his head at the broken stone, whispered, 'Did you see that? Drop dead, but the bloomin' Stone have broke eggsactly where Tusks done his pisho.'

Delusions of grandeur about the potency of Tusks' secretions had no place in the discussion under way round the broken dream.

Isaiah, as the professional where bereavement and mourning were concerned, was restoring morale. 'Now there's no need to worry and this is certainly not anybody's fault . . . right . . . right . . . hm . . . hm . . . ha and goodness me there's plenty more stones. We live in a land of stones . . . hm . . . hm . . .'

The Ffynon Druidion farmer and his wife and sons were also on the scene and the wife had no doubt at all they could, without delay, find a suitable Logan on their farm. Meanwhile, her husband guided the engine off the road and with crowbars and muscle, the aborted monster was heaved on to the greensward where it remains to this day.

The search for Logan Number Two was immediately successful but it was not until the following Saturday afternoon (Mr Lewis and his engine not being available during the week) that the steamer and trolley laden with the new stone of Proclamation chugged snail-paced in clouds of steam and fuss up Windy Hall Hill into Fishguard town. Here, Mr Lewis from Mathry village, cynosure of all eyes, spinning the steering wheel with self-conscious panache, made the final right-angled turn into the road that led to the site of the Bardic Circle.

As the little cortège marched that last hundred yards, with the crowd clapping and waving, the Reverend Isaiah's eyes began to stream, Schoolin's Adam's apple was gripped with the old familiar throb, the blacksmith's heavily lined smoky face had tiny giveaway

movements, John John the trapper openly snivelled and even the
juveniles wore expressions, wide-eyed and solemn and proud. The
stone was unloaded as sweet and easy as a truss of hay. Tea,
photographs, hand-shaking and then a harmonised rendering of
'Guide me O thou Great Jehovah', accompanied on the mouth
organ of a quarry worker, preceded the journey home where the
procession arrived to their own strains of 'Men of Harlech, March
to Glory'.

Though, as clerk to the Parish Council, Schoolin's principal
role was to minute the proceedings, this did not deter him from
taking an active part, and he often addressed the members at length
when his own favourite subjects were involved.

So it was that at the first meeting of the Parish Council after the
triumph of the Procession of the Logan, he was moved to rise,
forsake his role of clerk and, in the absence of Isaiah, the
Chairman, to address the assembly in his best oratorial style.

'It is very meet,' he said, 'that a Stone should have brought us
such great fame. For ours is truly a parish of stone. Our houses,
our farmsteads, our churches and chapels, they are all built of
stone. Our farm gates hang on stone pillars. Our cromlech on
Garn Llys hill, and the stones of Melus and Panus and the wife of
the knight Daar' – a reference to the ancient Christian memorial
stones found in use as gateposts on Llandruidion Farm and
brought for final resting in the church – 'and now this great Logan,
inscribed imperishably with the name of our village, will continue
to bear everlasting witness to our glorious heritage of stone.'

Even the minutes of the meeting were written in a style of
deep emotion.

'. . . the meeting is grateful to the Gorsedd Committee for giving St Nicholas the honour and privilege of providing the Logan Stone for the Gorsedd Circle and the St Nicholas people who took in the Stone were deeply moved by the enthusiastic welcome they received by the crowd assembled on Penslade on their arrival in Fishguard with the Logan stone.'

Two days before the opening of the 'National', the village contingent stood in the place of honour around the Logan, staring out to sea. In all, there were approximately five hundred people gathered from roundabout to witness the impending drama of the Great Arrival.

First sign was a smoke plume on the horizon and cries of 'There she is, there she is, over by there', and with surprising speed the red funnels, white super-structure and massive body of a trans-Atlantic liner bearing the American Eisteddfod expatriates hove into sight and entered the roadway of light laid down by the sun on Cardigan Bay.

One St Nicholas patriot felt especially strong emotion. Alone among those present, William Davis of Spring Gardens Farm enjoyed the distinction of having 'been to America', a unique status-enhancing honour in the Welsh countryside of those days. To have 'been to America' was the apotheosis of enterprise and adventure and in any discussion of a man's character and achievements, to have left out this crowning fact would have been unthinkable. William had returned from visiting his brother on just such a great ship.

The sound of the liner's engines grew louder until finally she moved with circumspection to the prescribed anchorage at the end of the breakwater. The 10,000-ton liner could proceed no further because the depth of water in the enclosed harbour was not

sufficient and this failure renewed the ache of an old Fishguard trauma which had never properly healed, especially with the retired sea captains and mariners. Octogenarian Captain Dai Morgan, six feet six inches tall and erect as a main mast, had spent forty of his fifty sea-faring years in sail, and he spoke for all present when pointing to the 'Cow and Calf' rocks beyond the headland, where the water was deep enough to berth the *Mauretania*. With a voice still holding the fog-horn power which had enabled him to be heard above the deep sea blast, he roared, striking his left palm with his right fist.

'Dammo, dammo. That's where the bloody breakwater should be. Down by there. Bloody shame. Fishguard could have been the biggest port for the American traffic. Dammo man, America is straight over by there . . .' and he pointed with a flourish across the darkening vistas of the bay. Endorsement came from Billy John, Fishguard boatswain, who had once enabled a dead captain to arrive home sweet enough for a Christian burial by pickling his body in rum inside a lead-lined casket.

He added the inevitable rider, though whether it was more than a rumour was never made properly clear, 'The G.W.R. engineer in charge drowned himself when he realised his mistake. Pity for him, poor bugger, but he was the one to blame.'

But for once, the grumbling of the old mariners awoke little echo, and the subject died as the returning exiles came home along the breakwater – 90 feet high above the bed of the sea, with 800 tons of rock blasted from the nearby Goodwick cliff for every foot – to nourish their roots in the compost of culture at the 'National', to enjoy the special status still accorded to those Welshmen who have prospered in America. Then the St Nicholas contingent returned to the village on foot, by bicycle, by horse and trap and in the Reverend Isaiah's 12 h.p. Morris which he drove through the narrow lanes with a certainty that his was the only car on the road – a paralysing experience for any passenger foolish enough not to close his eyes.

The following evening, the triumph of the Logan and the liner's arrival had been relived many times before Meiriog said, 'Let's have a song then, Telyn,' and led the way into the shadows of the resonant, low-raftered smithy for a Saturday night sing-song. Telyn, the ginger-haired, freckled farm labourer, stood by the anvil, accompanied again on the mouth organ concealed in the huge palm of the quarry worker, and sang 'David of the White Rock', 'Grandmother's Walking Stick' and other evergreens.

Then it was time for Schoolin, with a piece of circular iron rod as baton, to lead the group in the regular Saturday night hymns, moving his big-range baritone with synchromesh ease into tenor or bass as the choir balance demanded; until, with candles winking in cottage windows and open doors, the moment came for the ending piece of many Saturdays, and the sweetly mournful harmonies of Dr Parry's 'Myfanwy' rose and fell from the smoke-blackened welkin. It brought back memories (as it does still for some, after half a century) of a coal-pocked, white-faced group of miners from the rotting Rhondda valley, dressed in blue suits and white scarves, who had one night in the St Nicholas schoolroom, when touring rural Wales, sung it for coppers and bread as it had never been heard before.

None of the eighty choirs competing at the forthcoming 'National' next week in Fishguard would ever sing better than that, unless it was – once again – the choir made up of miners from the still rotting valleys. They were able to attend and compete at the Eisteddfod, thanks to a charitable donation of money for the purpose from the *Western Mail* in Cardiff.

CHAPTER NINE

Pride of Cemaes

'In view of the increasing number of cars in the parish it was decided to write to the Road Surveyor about widening the road.'
Minutes of the Parish Council Meeting, 20 April 1930

At two o'clock on a bright April day, the Shire stallion, led by Ishmael James, proceeded along the road between Llangloffan and the St Nicholas crossroads. It was Friday afternoon, the end of a dry week and the heavy entire lifted little clouds of dust on to blue violets and red cuckoo pint and pink butterbur and yellow and red primroses, as his hooves rang on the stony road.

No animal is more essentially male than the entire, and Pride of Cemaes was king of his kind. His head was small, yet arrogantly masculine. He stood 20 hands (80 inches) and now at the beginning of the season, before eighty mares and many, many more miles had taken their body toll, he weighed over a ton. ·Yet despite his bulk, his body was put together with such art that however he walked or stood or danced or reared, the posture or movement was sheer and faultless. His back was short and wide, ribs deep and widely sprung – giving him a tun-like girth – quarters wheat-sack wide, shoulders and thighs flat-boned, clean as a split baulk of oak. Hide gleaming like a conker, tail in a bun, bridle ribbon-edged, coronets and pasterns flinging snowy feather, he filled the lane with nuptial majesty.

As he approached the village he smelled the mare, his liquid eyes grew fierce, and lifting his head to the limit of the reins joined to his girth straps, he sent out a thrilling call, performed a jig of ardour, lifting his huge pedestal hooves until he was almost across the road. His groom chided him firmly back into line. With his entires, Ishmael never for one moment slackened the reins of control.

Ishmael worked as a carter at Pennybanc Farm for most of the year, but for three months he travelled the licensed stallion. Customers planned to foal their mares between March and June, and as they carried for about eleven months – a bit longer in early spring when the young foals seemed loth to come out and brave the March winds – Pride's main work was from April to July. Mares at grass were the most likely to conceive and hold.

Today, Pride's first rendezvous was with Puss, the grocer's dip-backed mare who spent her days racing from farm to farm, collecting rabbits, ending each round in a frantic rush to deliver on time to the train. With characteristic exuberance, Bilbow often ascribed Arabian ancestry to his fleet-footed but unlovely steed and had proclaimed his intention of one day marrying Shire strength to desert fleetness of foot.

'There's no reason at all why you shouldn't breed a horse that will plough at ten miles an hour,' he explained to the grinning carters.

On the morning for this splendid merger, poor Puss, the mythical Arab, looked more like a sacrifice than a bride, as her ton of gleaming suitor approached the yard where she was coralled.

Ishmael made a clicking sound of disapproval to himself when he took in the bony thin-legged, dip-backed mare. If Pride didn't

get there first thrust, and doubly smart at that, the mare could well go down. He held the entire back on the rein as, muttering savagely, the horse tried to quicken his pace, again throwing out that mating challenge, ears signalling eagerness, his gleaming body agog with ardour.

'Good morning, Ishmael.' Shirt-sleeved Bilbow, standing by the gate with an expression of importance, raised his hand in greeting.

The groom held the stallion back with an iron hand until the grocer opened the gate and stood a few paces inside. Pride began to surge forward and Ishmael barked urgently, 'Stand to one side, man, away from the mare.'

The warning was timely, for as Bilbow stepped aside, Puss, laying her ears flat, turned a flirtatious back and thumped the stallion in his gleaming ribs with a flying kick of both hind hooves, bit him on his arching neck and then stood stock still as he began to rear like a public statue brought to life. As Puss was covered, her legs, as Ishmael had feared, began to give and buckle but he was able to successfully hasten the grotesquely inappropriate mating. Puss just stayed on her legs.

Ishmael led out the snorting stallion, took him round the corner to the front of the shop, out of sight of the still excited Puss. Bilbow followed, and lit a new Woodbine from the stub of the old.

'How much do I owe you?' he asked, and then added, preparing as was his wont to soar into the strange world where he loved to travel. 'Did you ever hear about Bucking Cephalous? Now there was a horse. You see . . .'

Before Ishmael could reply or Bilbow begin to orate on the equine glory of the world conqueror's charger, a fiery-faced Aggie appeared at the door, towel in hand, as unmistakable in her intention as a cobra poised to strike. But whatever she had to say, stayed unsaid as she saw the entire, and she went back inside.

'Two pounds, please,' said Ishmael, and jerked his head in the direction of Puss around the corner, adding, 'If she dosn't hold, you can have another service free.' He pocketed the money and patted the stallion's mighty neck. 'But he settled sixty mares first service last year,' he said, and though he was convinced that her poor condition made it unlikely Puss would conceive, he held his peace. Miracles had happened before, and he had learned to keep his mouth shut.

(Alas, poor Puss, who should surely have had a few hours to rest and settle in a green paddock, was immediately sent racing through the countryside on her collection and delivery chores. Three weeks later she was in season again.)

Ishmael took out his turnip watch, formal indication of departure, touched his cap to Aggie, still dimly visible in the shadow of the shop, and led the stallion up the village street past the smithy. He returned the wave from the smith who was grinning mischievously in the direction of the grocer's shop. Ishmael glanced down at the entire's hooves, hidden beneath cascades of snowy feather. He would need the smith's services in less than two weeks' time, for stony roads played havoc with shoes. His gaze lingered a moment on the movement of the giant hooves, lifting and falling without effort as though on ball-bearings, a sweetness of gait which Pride had passed to scores of his progeny.

Free of the village, Ishmael and Pride fell into a rhythm of stride which appeared unhurried, but ate up the miles. As often, after the stallion had been working, Ishmael's thoughts took on erotic colour. He thought of some of the women *he* had possessed on his tours of duty: unable, or unwilling, to escape the bold, sultry invitation in the groom's sloe-coloured eyes – slightly squinted so they never seemed to release the snared object of their gaze – the promise of his big lips, red as rose hips in the snow, the appeal of the arrogant arching chest and the stalwart shoulders.

Then, as often happened, the smiling face of his dark-haired wife suddenly ousted the others. Betty never left him in doubt that she knew all about the weakness which had earned him the nickname in some quarters of Ishmael the Goat. But she had sense enough to know too that it didn't amount to a damn really, that she and the children were all that really mattered in his life.

Travelling up and down the country with Pride, the old sod made you feel randy yourself, and the nights away from home made you lonely, and when the two things came together – well, you took your pleasure when it came. He remembered the last time a raging Betty had taken him apart, pulled his beard till tears came, kicked his arse so he remembered it every time he sat down for days. She could read him like a book and when he came home after a few days on the road, his guilt was in his eyes as plain as the ribbon on Pride's bridle. But he'd try and take her a good present next time he stayed away.

Ishmael did not always travel on foot, for Pride's territory covered a radius of approximately twelve miles and for outlying farms he travelled with pony and trap. The stallion enjoyed the company of his little gelding companion in the same way that he enjoyed the presence of one of the farm cats in his manger at night. For these trips, Ishmael carried a supply of top quality crushed oats and meadow hay. The stallion needed the best if he was to stay at his peak and when he arrived back late at the stable after a service trip, usually on a Saturday evening, he gave Pride a good feed of warm bran mash to keep him comfortable during the Sabbath idleness.

Not that Pride had it all his own way. There were three other stallions on hire who paraded in finery to book orders at Fishguard Cattle Show and Mathry and Letterston Pleasure Fairs. But Pride's record ensured him as much work as he could handle.

Ishmael was jerked from reverie by a giant pull as Pride reared and simultaneously shied towards the grass verge so that, for a

moment, the groom was off balance and the stallion out of control. The bullnose Morris Cowley had come round the blind corner, juddering to a squealing halt not twenty yards away. Peering with white face through the windscreen was Mrs Reynolds (the tweedy daughter of Mrs Davies the aristocratic School Manager) from Trellys Farm where Pride had served a mare a week before. Fumbling with the control to put the car into reverse, she pushed the throttle instead of the clutch, the engine roared and gear cogs banged and screeched.

It was like putting a piece of gorse under the stallion's tail. 'Whoa now, boy. Whoa there, now . . .' Ishmael's order was a ringing bark, his hand on the bridle, iron. Still panicking, Pride began to drag his groom towards the car until Ishmael dealt him a sharp blow with his stick on his left flank, at the same time pulling hard on the bridle until Pride was facing in the opposite direction, and was led still cavorting and trembling away from the car. Ishmael took the stallion through the first field opening.

It was not the first time he had been forced to take Pride off the road. While two cars might just squeeze past at a wide point, no one cared to share the road with a passing stallion. The problem was becoming acute for there was now a total of six cars in the parish.

Ishmael reached his destination at half past four. There was no problem here. The mare and Pride were giants together. She had already borne three foals and the covering was easy and straight-forward. After a wash and tea and gossip in the farm kitchen, Ishmael was homeward bound by half past five. As groom and entire reached the second crossroads where the turning to the left led to his home six miles away, Ishmael took Pride a little way down the right fork, got out his little notebook of bookings and confirmed the stallion's appointment at Ton-y-Gefoil Farm for the following Monday.

It had been dimly at the back of his mind since setting off from Pride's last service that he might turn right here instead of left. He took out the gilt and enamel turnip given to him by his wife Betty for his forty-fifth birthday and, with the reminder of home, his decision for a moment hung in the balance. But it was six o'clock. It would be dark when he got home. A mass of cloud over Abermawr suddenly blacked out the sun and signs of rain piled up on the sea. The possibility he might not be welcome at the farm where the widow lived, never entered his head. It was now just a

question of whether it was prudent. The labourers left at half past five and would be back home by now. The coast was clear. Groom and entire began to walk down the lane to the farm.

Megan Nichols was standing before her bedroom mirror 'putting herself tidy' when she saw Ishmael leading the stallion towards the house.

Funny, she thought, he wasn't due till Monday when her head carter, William Roberts, had told her the mare would be on and the stallion was booked. Oh well, that was his problem. He'd just have to come back in two days' time. Then a sudden thought flashed through her mind, touched the throttle of her pulses and she drew a deep breath. The old goat. She knew all about Ishmael's reputation. What woman in the parish didn't?

She patted her hair, now as certain about what was going to happen as she was sure about the slightly heightened colour which her mirror revealed. She had been widowed for almost a year and missed the marriage bed, even though Jack had been thirteen years older than her. She examined herself in the glass. At fifty-two she was still a proposition for any mature man: complexion pink and white, no grey in her centrally parted raven black hair, hardly any lines in her neck, the whites of her green eyes clear, her breasts still plump and full. She cupped her left breast with her right hand and suddenly giggled as she remembered a ribald farm joke about dropped udders in elderly cows.

She could hear now the heavy tread of the stallion as Ishmael entered the yard and from behind the curtain watched the short, stalwart figure pause and tie the horse to the ring in the stable wall. She remembered having seen him parading the entire and taking orders at Letterston Fair.

The knock on the open top half of the kitchen door was firm, loud, confident. Megan came down through the hall, affected surprise and puzzlement when she met and was held by those eyes with their slight squint, as the groom doffed his cap with a suggestion of a bow.

'Evening, Mrs Nichols,' he said. 'I was just passing by. As I haven't seen William Roberts for a month, I just wanted to make sure everything was all right for Monday.'

The excuse was as transparent as a goldfish bowl, but she played his game, at the same time taking in the bold-featured face with the red lips and short beard, and now the cap-flattened curls, conscious suddenly that she could not escape those slightly adrift eyes, even had she wanted to.

'As far as I know, it's all right,' she replied. 'William hasn't said anything to me.'

Then she gave first voice to the decision which had been made as she had watched groom and stallion from the upstairs window.

'You've had a long walk, I suppose,' she said. 'Would you like to come in for a cup of tea?' She patted her hair.

The dusk was already beginning to seed the air as she opened the bottom half of the door.

'Sit down,' she said and drew an oak chair out from the table.

The kitchen was suddenly loud with the language of libido. Megan moved slowly to the solid fuel stove, stood a little further away than was strictly necessary to reach the shining brass-handled kettle so that her left breast was strained against her white jersey. Her intention was as plain to the experienced Ishmael as though she had announced it in words. She heard the movement of the chair, half-turned to find him so close that she either had to lean against the hot stove or press against him. He reached out two powerful hands and with surprising gentleness ran his palms softly across her ears and into her hair. His tone was tender and confident.

'I've fancied you,' he said, 'ever since I saw you riding on the horses at Letterston Fair . . .'

He pressed against her and began to draw patterns with his lips on her face, just touching the corners of her mouth with his titillating arabesques, gently at first and then with increasing passion, her black tresses still gathered in his hands, his beard following his mouth in a soft cascade of sensation.

Megan strained away for a moment and said, her face slightly flushed, as though she had been running, 'You don't waste much time, do you?'

Ishmael replied, 'I'll go and turn the stallion into the Home Ground. He won't hurt there and nobody will see him . . .'

He walked through the kitchen gloaming, a short upright, Pan-like figure, conscious of his own mastery of a familiar situation.

When he returned, there was a cup of tea on the table, but the kitchen was empty. He drank the tea before mounting the stairs.

There was no evidence of Ishmael's call when he led the stallion out at half past five the next morning and the pair were three miles away in the dew-drenched, bird-loud countryside before the first worker was abroad. The memory of Megan's body and the comfort and triumphs of the night stayed with him for the early part of the journey and then, as the morning matured, the figure of his wife began to intrude and bring unease. He pulled up for a moment by a gateway, to watch a sparrowhawk falling like a stone through the sky, vaguely conscious that the world was loud with birdsong. The old uneasy thought returned. If only he had been able to buy something to take home for Betty and the children.

As he turned to move away from the gate a figure reached the corner and came in view fifty yards away. William the giant fisherman. No one knew his surname, except Bilbow in the last

pensioned years of his life who, if asked, would undoubtedly
have asserted his inviolate duty under the Official Secrets Act or
some-such. William lived alone in a tiny beachside cottage, a few
pebbly paces from the old limekiln which had once processed
heaped tons of limestone carried by boat into Aberbach. This
brought galloping farmers in competing haste, for lime was scarce
in those horse-drawn days and it was first come, first served for
the precious boat-carried commodity which the hungry, sour
St Nicholas soil soaked up like a sponge.

When the winter gales made fishing impossible, the dark days
and nights closed round William and except for his once-a-month
visit to the shop for his pension, groceries, matches, candles and
tobacco, he saw and was seen by no one. During these months, he
lived on what fish the sporadical fine days allowed him to catch –
and especially on eels. The river that flowed sluggishly across the
moors, to emerge finally through the great Aberbach filter-bed of
blue pebbles, was a particularly rich source and when, obedient to
the mysterious summons of maturity, they donned their nuptial
livery and made for the nearby sea, William's traps were there to
intercept them and help stock his winter larder.

But March to October, or as early and late as wind and waves
allowed, he trapped lobster and crabs and, with the strength which
had become legendary, caught mackerel and other fish in the cork-
bobbing seine net which he hauled in unaided in Samson
feats of strength. This particular morning, he was on his way to
the village, with his wares in a shoulder-poised basket. The fierce
minatory fashion in which he placed his basket on the doorstep – as
though daring anyone not to buy – made everybody purchase,
almost out of fear.

Ishmael pulled up in the middle of the road as the giant approached, thick woollen stockings tucked into boots, huge torso encased in a heavy dark-blue oiled jersey, a woollen bonnet on his head; his beard was like white heather, the stringy, drooping moustache like broome grass.

'Morning, William.' Ishmael greeted the giant, with eagerness. 'You're just the man I wanted to see. Want to buy something for the missus. Something specially nice.' He tied Pride with his rope halter to the gatepost.

Wordlessly, fiercely, William deposited his heavy half-bushel basket on the road, reached down and lifted out from the top layer of seaweed, a monster of the rocky deep. The carapace was principally reddish yellow, but with opalescent flecks of blue as though it had been impregnated with the splendour of the Aberbach sea.

'One of the biggest I ever caught. Weighs four pounds. Two shillings.' His tone was almost contemptuous. There was no haggling with William. He held out his hand.

Ishmael was flooded with gratitude and relief, and love for his wife, as the guilt of the night ebbed into the morning. Lobster was her very best favourite and this was a real beauty, a proper feast. He moved across to Pride and took the sack which had carried yesterday's supply of crushed oats. He turned it inside out and shook out the dust. He paid his two shillings, tied another short piece of binder twine round the huge orange crusher claw and then the peace-offering – beaky predatory mouth chewingly open, long whiplash antennae held aloft like aerials, four pointed antennules a bristling barrage in front of the revolving stalk eyes – was stored in the sack.

William moved off with a reluctantly grunted farewell, huge, solitary, menacing, like some briny giant who had strayed from the deep world of whales and dolphins, while Ishmael strode home with a lighter tread, confident and comforted by the heavy peace-keeping weight on his shoulder.

Four days later, on a night of full moon, William Roberts, the head carter at Aber Farm – a short, wiry, fearless man in his fifties, who walked with a stride lengthened by hundreds of miles of horse work in the fields – reached the field gate above the cottage of William the giant fisherman, just before midnight. As he often did, when the day's toil seemed unending – and he had begun work at six o'clock that morning – he began to sing in a somewhat harsh baritone voice. The mare in the field turned towards the familiar sound, her almost white face and the dark-and-light-grey interweaving splashes with which nature had brushed her hide, agleam in the moon.

The carter's elegy about the heartache death of a famous black Welsh pig ended, and he stood a moment taking stock. In the two hours since he had seen her, the mare had changed. Her head, then held high, was drooping, her belly slightly asymetrical with its gravid load now looked even vaster and more pendulous in the moonlight. She appeared to be resigned, motionless, enveloped in a cocoon of massive ripeness, waiting, as most heavy mares seem to do, for midnight to pass before beginning to bring her foal into the world.

William moved to her head, tidied the forelock to one side, ran his hand down to the velvety lips.

'There, there, my beauty, there, there,' he spoke softly and to her alone.

She was comforted by his presence, but took his caresses passively, her usual responsiveness engulfed in the hormonal surge beginning to flood her womb, yet dimly, distantly. The carter's hand passed firmly along her shivering abdomen to the roots of the silvery tail where the hollows on either side were now deep enough to take his fist. Hand and voice moved down to the hard udder. She had been bagging up and exuding the waxy substance of pregnancy's end since a week previously and the gobbets were an inch long on the teats.

She could start any minute, he thought and, indeed, as his hand left her udder, the mare began to strain, passed a little water and wind and looked anxiously round towards her tail. Her back remained slightly arched, she began fidgeting, stamped her left front hoof on the earth, tilted her back right on edge for a moment, as though to rest. Then she began to fold her massive limbs, and the carter moved away as she lay down with a huge gusty sigh. A minute later she heaved herself upright, strained, put her head down as though to graze, pawed the earth with alternate front feet, and then lay down again.

William Roberts unbuckled the midwife's canvas bag which had belonged to the old boss, laid it open a few yards away, checked the kit: flask of hot water, soap, small hand towel, bottle of Condy's Fluid, two short lengths of cheese cloth, a pot of vaseline,

Stockholm Tar, a short piece of cord, and his own bottle of cold sweet tea. He began to worry. Perhaps he should have asked Mrs Nichols to get the vet in earlier on in the evening, to make sure everything was all right. Rhonwen had foaled four times before, without trouble, so he had let it go. But in the old days he always had the boss with him for foaling, and even so they had been forced to call in Captain Mathias of Llangwarren for two other mares during the last five years. Once the hind legs had been in front and bent at the hocks, and on another occasion the foal had been on its back.

As the tension-loaded minutes ticked away, Rhonwen's birth pangs and the straining grew stronger and more frequent, and after a short period of upright straining, she lay down again, her colossal body sprawled on the grass, epitome of the titan Shire in labour, awesomely huge, even to the carter who spent his life in the shadow of these gentle giants.

He washed his hands just as the liquid caul surrounding the foal in the womb burst, flooding the mare's passage with lubricating mucous. A minute later the feet appeared. Thank God! But relief was misplaced for the foal refused to be born. He smeared his hand with vaseline, stood by the mare, speaking words of comfort. It took determination and strength to get his right hand inside. He felt for the foal's head, following with his fingers along its hooves and pasterns, to the nostrils. Thank God, the foal was lying right. His arm was caught in the vice of the mare's contractions and was almost numb before he withdrew it.

Suddenly, despite his total concentration on the mare, he knew he was no longer alone. His head jerked round, as though drawn by an outside force and for a moment he experienced a scalp-crawling fear. The dark figure standing on the rise of the meadow was huge, motionless, menacing. The basket on the shoulder might have been a missile paused for launching. His back was to the moon and the bearded, heavily moustached face was only dimly discernible under the dark woollen bonnet. William, the giant recluse from the Aberbach creek, taking a short cut home from his mackerel fishing, had paused to take in the birth drama unfolding in the moon-silvered field.

He made no gesture or sound of greeting, and a loud groan from the mare as she laboriously stood up again brought the carter back to his task. Rhonwen was tiring, but more confident now that he could help, he wrapped the cheese cloth round the protruding slippery feet and, taking his time, from the rhythm of her pains,

E

began to pull strongly and steadily on the fetlocks backwards and
downwards towards the earth, maintaining his tension on the foal
in the intervals of relaxation between pangs. He was exerting
every ounce of his strength when the muzzle appeared above the
protruding feet. The passage began to widen and the mare gave a
huge groan as the big head slipped through, and in a few seconds
the foal was lying helpless, wet and shocked on the spring turf,
encased in the clinging caul which glistened in the moon. Rhonwen
had gone over her time by a week and the reason for the hard
birth was now clear. The foal was huge.

The tension drained away from the carter in a huge exhalation
of breath. He was sweating profusely, his hands were shaking and
his mouth was dry.

Rhonwen turned round to get at her foal and, in the process,
ruptured the birth cord, as Nature intended her to do. She began
to lick away the membrane from the foal's face which the carter
had already opened so the foal could take his first breath of sea air.
The mare began to clean and massage, nuzzling, pushing, licking.
When the foal was dry, William gently turned the defenceless
little giant – already comically bearded, and with a carpet-fringe
mane – on its side, squeezed out the residues of umbilical fluid
and dabbed the navel with Stockholm Tar. Pride's first foal of
the year was a colt.

A movement caught the corner of his eye. The fisherman who
must have watched the giant birth right through was striding out
for home.

The mare began again to push and nuzzle to get the colt to
his feet, pausing from time to time to stare and admire with a soft,
maternal expression, before resuming her duties with energetic
solicititude. It took carter and mare an hour to get the colt so he
could just wobblingly stand. He cleared the teats of wax, coaxed

and cajoled the baby to the udder, placed a teat in his mouth. With surprisingly greedy strength, he began to suck the precious first beestings which would clear his baby stomach of sludge.

The job was finished. He made a final check. The mare was near water, the night warm, the site sheltered, the foal had drunk, there was spring grass for the mother to graze. He would check her for cleansing on his way to work in the morning. He patted the massive neck. 'Well done, my old love,' he said gratefully and put his cheek against hers for a moment. With a glance at the sky, he decided to suggest to Mrs Nichols they should call the colt Moonlight. He yawned hugely, took a long swig of his favourite drink of cold tea. He looked at his Ingersoll. It was three o'clock.

Suddenly, as though she had just remembered her manners, the mare lifted her head, now once again her old statuesque, majestic self as she stood posed in the moonlight, looked in the carter's direction, and gave out the loud ringing greeting of her kind. He smiled, and began the walk home. He clicked his tongue disapprovingly as, breasting the rise into the new ley, he saw the scores of rabbits nibbling the precious clover. He clapped his big hands together and shouted to send the little devils scurrying for the field banks. He was grateful for the continuing brightness of the midwife moon to ease the journey home, dimly conscious of the sound and swing of the sea breaking with splashy gentleness on the shore. He could just see the fisherman's cottage, its brown distempered walls glowing like gingerbread in the moonlight.

He began to sing softly the sad saga of the black Welsh pig, but got no further than the first verse. For once he was too tired even to sing.

He saw the little heap on his cottage doorstep when he was twenty yards away. In a bed of seaweed, protected by a little carefully constructed cromlech of flat stones, he uncovered twelve newly caught mackerel, their scales agleam in the light of the moon – a tribute from another tradesman of the night.

CHAPTER TEN

Ring of Iron

'It was proposed and seconded that the blacksmith place a section in the war memorial railing.'

Minutes of the Parish Council Meeting, 22 April 1932

At seven o'clock, Meiriog, the third-generation St Nicholas blacksmith, unlocked the padlock which secured the half-doors of his blacksmith's shop and pushed them open. The smithy was a small stone-built room with low slate roof, the roughly mortared interior walls dark with the grime of almost a century of family blacksmithing, recesses littered with discarded iron tools, pensioned-off drills, worn-out bellows, sundry lengths of iron. The floor was beaten earth and cobble stones, the shop lit by three small windows, and a fixed skylight which was virtually opaque. It was a cold crepuscular world smelling of dead ash, water scummed with red scale, horse droppings and the lingering tang of burnt hoof.

The smith tied on his leather apron, and with the small fire-hook and soft hand brush cleaned the ash and clinker from the firepot in the circular brick-built hearth. He placed a handful of oily wood shaving on the nozzle of the bellows pipe, arranged small lumps of coal on top and as the lit shavings began to flare, fed the infant flame with tiny precision whiffs of air from the bellows until a live bed was formed. He banked the fire on three sides with green freshly mixed culm, leaving an empty space directly opposite to receive the horseshoes, which he placed on the anvil.

He walked to the door, a small wiry figure with a smoky complexion and seamed face, a notorious gossip with darting brown eyes which could sparkle with mischief and malice. He looked down the road. He liked to watch the horses approaching, especially if they were first timers to the smithy, for the horse's gait might indicate a defect needing adjustment. He had several 'specials' on his books, like Bronwen the Trefelgarn shire which had 'forging' feet which made her strike the back of a front hoof with the toe of a hind. He cured this with lighter concave front shoes to lengthen the front stride, and heavier shoes behind which shortened her back stride.

The man approaching was Clogs' father, dressed in carter's 'uniform', yellow corduroys, yorked below the knees with binder twine, Welsh striped flannel shirt closed with a stud, an aged cloth waistcoat, faded blue denim jacket, and oilskin coat. Like all the parish carters, he was small in stature, typical of the soft-spoken catalysts who controlled the horsepower on the farms.

Greetings over, he pointed to the mare's front hoof. 'The mare's lost a shoe. Meant to bring her in last week but we were hauling dung and wanted to finish.'

Meiriog nodded, and turned to go inside. 'Bring her in. Everything's ready.'

Shoeing a placid mare like Maggie was a simple, if physically demanding drill – not like a stallion where the leg was heavy as a tree and your concentration could never waver, or shoeing a colt which could be a hard rough business. Meiriog lifted the heavy legs in turn and performed the routine tasks: the old shoes removed, the hooves trimmed, pared, and cleaned of a faintly malodorous, chalky substance. He touched up the fire and while the shoes were heating in the blaze, the smith retrieved an extinguished half cigarette from the sill, lit up from a tongs-held glowing coal, and jerked his head in the direction of the shop.

'I hear his nibs came home in style last night.' he said, showing discoloured teeth in a malicious grin. He waited a moment, whetting the appetite of his audience who couldn't have heard the story.

'Seems he took on a load at the Farmers' Arms and couldn't get home. So the Fowlman brought him back. He'd been with a load of cocks and hens to market. Trouble was, his van's got no back seat, just shelves, so they took off Bilbow's boots, lifted him into the back and pushed his legs through between the shelves to the front, put his boots back on and sent him home with his head poking through the back and his feet by the Fowlman's earole.'

The blacksmith drew heavily on his cigarette, accompanied a loud snorting chuckle with a twin stream of smoke through flaring nostrils.

'When he arrived outside the shop, they couldn't get him out. The Fowlman had to get Mrs Bilbow's help and after taking off his boots it took the two of them pulling hard to slide him through.'

Clogs' father gave a loud laugh as Meiriog finished his shopkeeper saga. Though he was a deacon, he liked a good story and besides, the grocer was a heretic and deserved to be trounced.

'Like a bloody eel from Abermawr,' he said, and threw back his head and laughed.

The story was over, malice savoured, shoes ready. The smith took the first from the fire with his tongs, tapped it on the anvil to remove scale, laid it on edge and with carefully timed blows from the wedge-end of his four-sided Catshead hammer, hammered out a thin leaf-shaped skin of iron for the clip. He reheated the shoe, impaled it lightly with a punch, placed it near at hand on the floor. With the mare's ponderous front leg held easily between his knees, checking the fit by the toe-clip, he applied the burning iron to the pared hoof, lightly to begin with and then intermittently with on and off pressure until the horn began to sizzle and throw out green pungent clouds like some Luciferan snuff. Each hoof was burned, and final shoe titivations made on the anvil before they were ready to nail.

Nailing on horse shoes, his big calloused hands acquired an eloquent sensitivity. The shoeing smith – the only craftsman to do so – has to work with living material, the horn which receives the nails is small, the quick near. Never any gossiping or straying attention now. With the shoe held in position with fingers and palm, Meiriog placed the first of the seven, slightly curving,

soft-metalled horseshoe nails into the second hole from the heel.
He began to hammer, feeling and exploring with his fingers for
the emerging point and then hammering home the nail head as far
as it would go, bending the end before twisting it off with the
claw of the small shoeing hammer.

The day's first shoeing was over by eight o'clock. There was
already another horse waiting outside. The smith straightened his
back, and David Evans the carter slowly backed his huge placid
mare into the daylight for the journey home.

As the ringing of the second mare's newly shod hooves retreated
down the village street, the smith lit another cigarette from a live
coal, drew a little culm to the base of the fire, and administered
a few whiffs from the bellows.

A child appeared in the doorway. In his right hand he held what
looked like a metal puzzle which the smith quickly realised was a
twisted hoop. The child was not a regular in the village and for a
moment the smith failed to place him. Then the close family
resemblance to his father – and mother – provided the clue. It was
Huw Owen who attended school in the next parish.

As the blacksmith took in the little gnome, frightened and alone
in the doorway, his cheeks smudged with runnels of tears, he
recalled the harsh sinister gossip which seven years previously had
greeted his birth in the promiscuously over-crowded cottage four
miles away and suddenly he felt a great pity for the child.

Drawing a heavy forearm across his moistening nose, he pinched-off his half-smoked Woodbine on the window ledge, held his big calloused hands in the air in mock astonishment and asked in a tone of gentle exaggeration, 'Is that your *hoop*?' His head held a little on one side, he added, 'What happened to it then?'

The tense solemn expression remained unchanged, the quivering movement of the lips was only just discernible.

'Steamroller,' came the whisper.

'*Steamroller*?' the smith echoed in genuine surprise. 'Steamroller? Did it go over it, then?'

There was a tiny nod.

'Well, in that case, we'll have to make you a new one, won't we?'

He moved to the doorway and took possession of the ruined hoop.

'Now let me see.' He took the child's hand, held it at a measured distance from the ground, his movements eloquent with restraint. He said, 'Your're a big boy now, so we'll have to make you a bigger hoop than the old one, won't we? We'll do it straightaway, shall we? Eh?'

He selected a length of round rod from the outside pile, took it inside, put one end in the fire, and returned to his little customer.

'I'd like you to help,' he said, and picking the boy up with the ease of a feather, placed him on the elm baulk, put the tiny hand on the bellows handle, covered it with his own and, careful to avoid pressing too strongly on it, began to blow – 'Nice and steady, nice and steady,' he intoned, and his voice took on a tuneful sing-song note as the little helper's arm was taken up and down by the handle of the leather bellows which – five feet high with six leather folds and looking like the cobwebby concertina of a giant – began to groan, creak, whistle and gust.

The smith heated both ends of the rod, thickened each extremity on the anvil, returned the rod to the fire and then holding the glowing wand in his tongs, began with delicate glancing blows to form the hoop, without denting or distorting the iron – a true test piece of old-fashioned blacksmithing – until, with both ends overlapping from the already near-perfect circle of iron, he dropped it over a selected mandril which was shaped like an old Welsh stovepipe hat and used for trueing his numerous rings and iron tyres. The lumpy extremities of the hoop, brought to white heat, were hammered together in a weld, which was shaped and rounded with a special tool, and finally polished on his foot-operated emery wheel in a screeching shower of red and gold sparks.

Taken up with a task which demanded total concentration, the smith almost forgot the customer who, standing on the bellows throne, was translated suddenly to a world of fire and iron and water, of strange primordial smells and swift noisy action, and the event had passed like a dream.

Meiriog picked up the driving hook which the steamroller had spared and put it in the little boy's right hand. They went to the door. Huw took his other hand from his trouser pocket, opened a closed fist and revealed two warm sixpenny pieces.

Meiriog took one, closed the little boy's fingers over the other, and crouched to whisper conspiratorially into his ear. 'One for me and one for you – for peardrops,' he said. He gave a big wink and a smile.

He straightened up and his smile changed to a scowl. Old Margiad Evans, the biting castrator's mother, was standing a few yards away, staring at the little boy.

'Good morning, blacksmith,' she said.

He brushed his nose with a hairy wrist. 'Morning,' he answered grudgingly. He couldn't stand the interfering old bitch.

She continued to stare, and now with malice shining in his eyes, the smith took the hoop and hook and ran a little noisy trial course round the old woman, his fifty-five years falling away in a cheeky tease.

'There, she's running lovely,' he told his customer, ignoring the gossip. 'Now, I want you to run your hoop as fast and straight as you can to the shop.'

Huw suddenly remembered his father's last, strongly worded injunction.

'Thank you, sir,' he whispered.

With mighty concentration, determined to make this the best run of his life, he engaged his new hoop in the driving hook and after a few wobbles, ran straight and true to Bilbow's store.

The smith turned to go back to the smithy.

'Who was that?' the old woman asked like a snapping turtle.

He paused, waited long enough for her to wonder whether he was going to reply.

'That was little Huw Owen,' he said eventually. 'Lovely little boy.'

Margiad's nose lengthened, her bony chin ran to a sharp point, her eyes oozed spite. '*Owen*,' she hissed, '*Owen*. I thought so. What right has he got to that name anyhow, I'd like to know. Ugh a fi.' Her dewdrop grew to fruition. 'Read Leviticus, it's all in Leviticus,' she shrilled.

The smith restrained a strong urge to spit in her direction as, from the corner of his eye, he saw her son William emerging from the house, wearing his usual melancholy expression. He mounted his bicycle and rode towards nearby Parsonage Farm for his first boar-biting stint of the day.

As he nodded and went past, a thought entered the smith's mind which suddenly burned up his irritation, turned the annoyance and dislike in his face into an expression of unholy glee. Eyes brimming with mirth and malice, as they not infrequently were, he addressed the old woman.

'I was just thinking, Mrs Evans bach. What a lovely morning for a mouthful of pig's balls. Some mothers' sons get *all* the luck.'

But his lips did not move, the *coup de grace* remained in his mind. After all, he was the rector's church warden. He took out

his red spotted handkerchief, blew his nose with a trumpeting sound in her direction and, grinning and chuckling enough for two blacksmiths, escaped into the gloom of the smithy. He was still chuckling when his aged father arrived from the cottage he shared with his daughter, and walked slowly to the polished elm baulk where he passed the days with his dimming memories.

The two hardest physical stints performed by the smith during the year in the servicing of the one hundred horses on his books were the shoeing of the travelling stallion and the shoeing of Duke, a gigantic dappled grey gelding who stood taller even than Pride of Cemaes. Duke's monstrous hooves demanded the making of special shoes with two toe clips. His collar measured a record-breaking 38 inches from the top of the forewale to the throatpiece, one of the biggest ever made in Britain. Strong as a dinosaur, mild as a lamb, brainless as a waterfall, Duke travelled with the last of the horse-drawn threshing machines still operating in the parish.

The week before Duke signed his own death warrant with the spectacular flourish which was his natural style and had the sentence confirmed, as it were, by the smith, the cumbersome outmoded thresher had been pulled into the smithy for repairs and Meiriog had brought it as near good working order for the beginning of the season as its aged innards would allow. There was still a demand for its services, because the fee for a day's threshing was barely more than half that of the steam set of tackle.

One noon on a Thursday, the machine creaked and groaned into the small corn haggard of the weak-stomached William Evans, the parish castrator, to thresh out his one rick of barley for winter grist. The cloud of dust and chaff had settled, and the hum and roar of the belts was silenced before dark.

Mr Phillips, the threshing contractor, a tall cadaverous man, with long fluttering hands and an anxious face, decided to move on the following morning to his next assignment, so he fed a little hay to the horses, and cycled home, The night looked fine, but at seven o'clock the St Nicholas skies were torn apart by a thunderstorm, and an inch and a half of rain turned the world into a morning quagmire.

Duke had spent much of his working life waiting, tied to the back of the machine as an emergency reserve, for the threshing drum was normally pulled by two Shires, except when, as it did this morning, the deadweight of the old iron-wheeled machine defied their combined power. As the horses plunged and strained, the iron wheels sank lower into the chocolate mud of the gateway. Duke dozed with bowed head and tilted hoof, resting in peaceful ignorance, tied to a nearby hawthorn.

The owner walked round the machine, pushed his trilby to the back of his head and said with obvious reluctance to the sympathetic but ineffectual Mr Evans, 'Dammo' and 'Dammo' again, 'We'll have to use the Duke.'

So the two regulars were unharnessed and the gigantic reserve led forward, giant hooves lifted fastidiously high in the dark squelching mud. While he was being harnessed, the huge collar hoisted upside down over his head, the tug chains fastened and checked, the smallholder stood in front of the blinkered giant holding the reins firmly in both hands.

The owner approached and took over the reins. 'Whoa now, Duke boy,' he said nervously, and then again, 'Whoa now, my old babby . . .'

He took a final look at the bogged wheels, made a quick visual check on the couplings and then gave the command, 'Now then, my old babby, giddup hup by there . . .'

Duke's ears were laid flat on his mane, a tremor passed through his gigantic dappled frame and he attempted to move forward. The harness took a terrifying strain, the old threshing box shuddered and rocked and juddered but remained stuck in the mud. Then Duke's tree-trunk back legs, plastered with muddy feather, began plunging and pumping in the mud like enormous jacks, his sack-wide cruppers spread and tensed and sprouted corrugated sheets of muscle. He strained forward until he was a few feet off the ground. The wheels began to rock, the machine rattled and moaned and with squelching slowness began to shake and move forward inch by inch through the ruts. As Duke's front legs staggered to a solid foothold, he seemed to draw the rest of his body forward by their leverage, and this time the machine suddenly became free and lurched forward.

It was then that Duke made a huge violent swerve to the right, catching the owner unawares, so that he lost his hold on the reins. There was a noise of smashing wood, the machine won clear and with the world suddenly before him, the brainless giant took the machine at a great wheel-scrunching pace down the road, the threshing box pouring dust like a broken biscuit bag, until Duke was caught and dragged to a halt. Jerking the wooden brake-blocks on to the wheels, the owner ruefully surveyed the damage. He shook his head, muttered several 'dammo's', unharnessed the Duke and the waiting Shires and took the thresher up the village street to the blacksmith's shop.

Meiriog finished nailing the last shoe on the bay gelding before he came into the autumn sunlight to inspect the damage. He walked round and stopped where the stone pillar had caught and stove in the main side panel. He pulled out a piece of broken wood, made a loud clicking noise with his tongue and teeth as he saw the bent reciprocating sieves, and the two cracked cast iron cogs.

'You've cracked the drive,' he said with a frown. 'I don't know what I can do about that. They're cast. I can straighten out the sieves, though they'll never be quite right again. You'll never get any more spares for this old sod.'

He walked round to the back where the date 1897 was still just visible to underline his pessimism.

And so, after hearing Meiriog's diagnosis, Mr Phillips decided to wind up his fast-ebbing horse-drawn threshing business and the old machine was pensioned off to moulder away in his rick yard. Two months later, poor unemployed Duke, greatest of all the gentle giants, was led uncomplainingly up a ship's gangway in Cardiff and sent to Belgium. Here he was progressively drained of blood by an electric pump over a period of time and then, almost too weak to stand, had his throat cut and was sold as white stewing veal to working-class restaurants in Ostend.

The smith occupied a white-washed cottage with grey mortar-washed roof which was attached to the smithy. Though it was handy, particularly in winter, to live on top of the work, the living quarters were very cramped. The length of smithy and cottage were equal, as though half the intended house had escaped to form the forge – with just two small rooms down and two up, and the latter were more in the nature of lofts under the rafters than bedrooms proper.

The smith's wife, Martha, was a lady with grey elfin locks and a blacksmith's complexion, but she kept the cottage like a new pin, and cosy as the forge could become on those wet winter days when the top half of the stable door was tight closed, the fire a blaze of bellows-fed yellow flame and the rain buzzing like a swarm of bees on the black skylight.

If one passed Meiriog's cottage round half past six in the evening as he opened the front door, ready to occupy his straight-backed Welsh settle for the day's main meal, one would inhale a fierce savoury wind of Welsh broth which escaped into the street from the big black iron crock permanently agog with vegetables from Meiriog's garden. At the eye of Martha's swedey, cabbagey storm was sometimes a bit of beef (salted) from the butcher's cart, occasionally a boiling fowl, but always a piece of salty bacon from the annually fattened pig. Martha's philosophy was well known from constant repetition whenever the question of food came up – 'You can't 'ave a blacksmith working all day without plenty of packing, so I always makes sure Meiriog eats full of his *crombil*,' thereby crediting her husband with a gizzard.

Meiriog was principally concerned with shoeing, pointing ploughshares, sharpening harrows and other repairs to farm machinery, but he was involved in the day-to-day chores of the village and parish in a hundred ways essential to its life-style. He mended school desks and windows, made and repaired hinges for garden gates, scrapers to remove mud (in pre-rubber boot days) from hob-nailed boots, clamps to hold down corrugated iron sheds rattling and rippling in Atlantic gales, knob-ended pokers, chains to suspend kettles and saucepans, endless bastard-size nuts and bolts and pins, gate fasteners, fenders, coal tongs, hooks from which to hang pigs for cutting up, and to hold the joints of bacon and ham in the kitchen beams. He fitted iron tyres on wheel-barrows, put new handles in spades and shovels and mattocks and pickaxes and sickles and billhooks and axes, cut threads, bent pipes, set saws, patched coal scuttles, sharpened knives, and opened up the memorial railings to refurbish the names of the parish war dead.

He was, too, intimately involved in community affairs, was on the Parish Council for years, apart from being the rector's warden. His voice and opinion carried authority with old and young. Indeed, from time to time, members of the younger generation

felt the authority of his strong right arm – literally. They so respected its power, that if a fight had been arranged between some of the older boys, when the school peck order was being reshuffled or put to the test, there had to be an elaborate roundabout journey to the traditional bloody nose rendezvous in Parson's Lane which was about fifty yards from the smithy, for if the peace-keeping Meiriog suspected what was going on, he arrived at the double with his shirt tucked back over brawny forearms, a figure of power and menace, and seizing both contestants painfully, each by the ear, with his strong smith's fingers, he would threaten to bang their stupid heads together if they didn't immediately desist and shake hands: which was an entirely appropriate technique of peace-keeping for one who was both a sinewey smith and a church warden.

Over the years, nothing seemed to change in the smithy, which more than any other village institution epitomised the constancy of its life style, in those self-sufficient days. On long, lazy afternoons the ring of iron, heard throughout the village, was a curiously comforting sound.

The smithy served a double role in St Nicholas. Apart from its being a centre of craft, it had also taken over the role of the inn, forbidden by the Squire.

For the unattached young village males, summer evenings offered a choice of bored propinquity and stale gossip. As they sat together on the stone window sills of the grocer's shop, they provided a gauntlet of undressing eyes and ribald tongues, calculated to daunt all but the most intrepid female passerby.

Or there was a game of quoits or rounders in the school playground, or sing-songs and anvil-lifting trials of strength at the smithy. The blacksmith's shop was warm in winter, cooled by through draughts in summer, rich with primordial smells, and if the smith was working late, there was a feast for the eye as he deployed tools virtually unchanged for a thousand years, exploiting the self-regenerating power of rhythm with unrivalled elegance and economy of style, expressing his skill in certain judgements of hand and eye which hardly ever made use of rule or calipers.

The smith loved gossip and the stag sessions in the smithy would have put the most addicted tittle-tattling group of village women into distant second place. Made to measure for the audience, too, were the two little alcoves where spectators could stand without impeding the action which moved between fire, anvil and the cooling trough. The smithy craft centre was gossip shop, glee-club and, at its lowest common denominator, a place where the young men could gather and grumble and spit on the floor at the boredom of a publess village life.

CHAPTER ELEVEN

Smell of Summer

*'It was decided that the School should close for the
Summer holidays from July 27th to August 31st 1925.'*

School Managers' Minutes, 16 July 1925

As summer moved towards the school holidays, the village was
besieged by the grassy armies of Parc Davis and a dozen other
hayfields with which the village was surrounded. As they crept
closer and threatened to invade the houses, the hedgerows rioted
with colour: red and white campions, bright blue cluster flowers
of tufted vetch, silky white silverweed, rosy dove's-foot crane's bill,
buzzing forests of cow parsley, umbels of hemlock, corn marigolds
and ox-eyes and tansies and spear-plume thistle and comfrey and
bindweed and woody nightshade and figwort, foxglove and yellow
rattle and sowthistle and buttercups. The hayfields waved and
rustled, the air was filled with flying seed and spores of pollen,
and hosts of butterflies haunted the weeds.

Each day it seemed, the sun passed higher and hotter over the
village, so that by ten o'clock on this summer Saturday, the sweets
were already glistening in Bilbow's window, made smudgy by the
mouths and noses of the window shoppers.

A distant figure appeared, walking up the road, and the freckled
face of Clogs materialised. He had a smug expression plastered
over his normally sly look and from time to time broke into
snatches of provocative whistling to underline possession of a
secret. Collars Morgan, intolerant of any hint of uppityness, set

about blowing him into line with a derisively hooted 'Up your pipe then . . .' But Clogs continued his whistling progress along the road to his cottage. He reappeared a few minutes later, wheeling his ancient mudguardless bike with the huge wheels, and eating a bun.

Collars condescended to ask, 'Wot's up then, Clogs. Where you been then? Wotcha know?'

Clogs took a bite, gagging himself of further speech until he had brought the chew of pap and currants under control with a huge swallow which pushed his head forward like a turtle's and closed his eyes.

Finally, as Collars was preparing direct action with a little twisting, he offered, 'I been down Parc Davis.' He took another bite and Collars waited for the swallow even more impatiently.

Clogs went on, 'Davis is going to put a cow to the bull. When 'e stops cuttin'. My uncle said so.' Then he added, 'The rabbits is dying like flies, millions and millions of 'em.'

'Why didn't you say so you daft twit,' said Collars. 'If you'm a liar,' he added automatically, 'I'll give you a clip on the earole if 'e aint.'

He mounted his bike and hooting 'every egg a bird', the group rode down in his wake to Parc Davis. By the gate Sian the wall-eyed collie was safely tied with a piece of binder twine. Richard, Clogs' uncle, a tall cadaverous bachelor, who sang a lot but spoke little, was filing the triangular teeth of the mowing knife into silvery-blue sharpness, tapping in loose rivets and humming 'The Ash Grove', in which cadence and rhythm came and went with the file.

Shirt-sleeved, trilby-hatted William Davis was mowing with

his two Shires, Prince and Captain. The boys watched him
pull the team into line at the far end of the field and as the
sweat-lathered geldings approached where they stood, the world
was filled with the noisy whirl of reciprocating blades, tumbling
the birds'-foot trefoil, kidney vetch, sweet meadow grass, red and
white clover, crested dogs'-tail, yarrow, plantain, cowslips,
ryegrass, like a wave on the Abermawr shore.

'Whoa now, whoa!' William drew the horses to a halt, and
raised the heavy knife cradle off the ground into the upright
position with effortless strength. He pulled the sweating,
crowding geldings through a stationary right angle, backed the
machine a few feet, lowered the knife cradle with a clatter into the
ground-hugging position, cracked the oiled black reins on
glistening rumps and as the tug chains strained against the pole
and the gearing in the fluted wheels began to crackle, the orderly
holocaust of flowery grass began again.

Collars turned to Clogs and said accusingly, 'Where's they
rabbits and things you said got copped then?'

As he spoke, two rabbits, white-tufted tails upright, burst out
of the uncut grass and disappeared with a jinking run into the
hedgerow. Collars' right arm changed into a gun which shot them
both stone dead. His success took his mind off Clogs, and they
stood watching the mowing machine until it began to turn again
at the far end of the field. The sweet, sensual smell of cut grass
and flower stems hung in the air as the mowing machine
approached, with William Davis keeping a vigilant eye on the
swathe, ready to pull up the knife to avoid damage from lurking
stones. He was bouncing slightly on the sack-cushioned perforated

metal seat set in the springy column. He had been mowing since six o'clock in order to get well ahead before the flies began to torment the lathered horses. He repeated the field-corner turning routine, but this time locked the heavy knife into the vertical position, moving the horses forward to the new swathe before pulling them finally to rest. He left the reins slack so Prince and Captain, reeking with sweat, could pick up mouthfuls of the mown grass, eating awkwardly with green juice falling from velvety lips.

He said to Richard Evans, 'We'll give the horses five minutes' rest, then I'd like you to take over.' He measured the uncut grass with an experienced eye. 'We should just about get it finished by teatime.' William took in the group of boys outside the gate and raised his eyebrows.

'Well, well,' he said, 'you got nothing to do this morning, then. Couldn't you be carrying water from the well for your mothers, hey?'

He turned again to Richard, to confirm Clogs' statement.

'I'm going along now to put Blossom to the bull. She was coming on this morning and should be about ready. Then I'll have something to eat. I'll send Miss Davis down with a drink.'

William Davis walked off and when he had turned the corner, Collars Morgan, bent double, ran along the churchyard wall, minions behind. He reached and unlatched the iron gate and they moved through the cemetery, furtive as body snatchers, to the point overlooking the Spring Gardens yard, where they hid behind the gravestones.

There was a sound of bellowing, the rattle of chains from the cowshed and a White Shorthorn, udder swinging, came trotting

into the yard. Mr Davis went into the loosebox and emerged, leading the massive white-faced red-bodied bull, with a pole clipped to his nose-ring. The bull moved slowly and quietly, like an old professional, and then, lifting his head and wrinkling his lips and nose, gave a series of high-pitched bellows. William led the Hereford towards the white cow who waited until the bull was reached towards her with his nose and then trotted away to the other side of the yard. Mr Davis followed, with the now impatient bull pulling strongly on the staff.

Checking the gate was securely latched, Mr Davis unhasped the guide-pole from the nose-ring and gave the bull his freedom. Dewlap swaying, lips and nose wrinkling at the wafts of heat, the bull broke into a lumbering trot, his tumbling diapasons of ardour punctuated by hiccups of expelling air. Despite his bulk, he moved lightly by the cow's side until she was cornered by the gate. Five minutes later, stertorous and protesting, he was returned to his pen, and the back-arching Shorthorn was back in the byre.

Collars Morgan led his crouching gang through the churchyard and for a moment put Llewelyn on his back for a ribald mating mime, his bony knees on the younger boy's thin upper arm almost making him cry with pain. He got onto his bike with a shout of 'Abermawr, follow me or I'll kill yer,' and they pedalled out of the village, yelling like dervishes.

While William took a belated breakfast, his tall, bespectacled spinster sister Amelia, who had been a schoolmistress and spoke with a refined English accent, went into the dairy to draw the promised drink for Richard. She had taken to a country retirement like a robin to its territory, and loved the life. She brewed beer three times a year – for sheep shearing, haymaking, and the corn harvest – and the perfectionist approach which turned her quickly into one of the best butter-makers in the county had made her home-brewed beer famous.

Miss Davis made her own malt, spreading some of William's best barley inside a large earthenware crock and covering it with well water. She left it to soak for three days after which, still wet, it was spread over several trays, covered with butter muslin and placed in the inglenook. Here the soaked berries threw out a mass of tiny worm-like sproutlets which were dried slowly at the far end of the big hob. After sieving off the sweet, crispy, chewy culms, the malt was ready to give the full body and dark brown colour to her beer. (Few hops were used since the workers preferred a dark, sweet ale.) Her brewing utensils were simple; one large crock in which the well water was boiled over the everlasting culm fire, a brewing tub with a spigot, and a cask.

Her beer was ready for drinking inside a fortnight, after the introduction of the yeast, floated onto the mixture on a piece of toast; spicy, dark, rich and strong with a head like the frothing barm itself. It was however too early in the day for beer drinking and Miss Davis took Richard a jug of cold sweet tea. In any case, William had a rule that no beer was drunk while mowing was in progress. But there would be enough to spare for everybody once the actual harvesting began.

For although he was a deacon, William Davis was fond of his tipple and as often as not rode home in the trap from Thursday

151

market in Fishguard with slack reins and nodding after his lunch at the Farmers' Arms. As one who owned his own farm he was free of the teetotal writ that burdened the Squire's tenants.

Parc Davis was all mown by afternoon milking time, as William had forecast, and the long lines of wilting herbage remained untouched the next day, for nobody did other than essential chores, like feeding and milking, on Sunday. Indeed, nothing that could be done on Saturday to prepare for the Sabbath was ever neglected: additional water carried from the well, extra sticks cut, cows placed in fields where they could be brought in for milking without meeting church or chapel goers, fodder and meal put ready for pigs and hens.

But early on Monday, with the sun beating down, the dewless swathes were turned with long ash-handled hay rakes, with William Davis and his carter moving through the crop, rakes held lightly as flutes. They changed grip instinctively, according to whether swathes lay left or right, handles sliding through their palms like silk, rake heads never lifted. The following day, the swathes were tossed and loosed with pitchforks and left in rows to cure for another twenty-four hours.

Emrys the carpenter, who had lived a long village craftsman's life among mountains of redolent shavings from ash, oak, elm, Archangel Red, pitch pine, larch, spruce, the smell of linseed oil and paint, the fug of hot glue, and who had fashioned twenty superb wagons for the farms about, was walking slowly across to the smithy when he saw William Davis on his way to the field. William pulled up in the hay wain Emrys had made and, getting down, lifted out the heavy can. He arrived in time to catch the wink and the familiar words between the smith and the farmer, part of an annual ritual of haymaking hospitality.

'A drop of buttermilk today, my lad, straight out of the churn,' and William pulled the can lid up with a plop and filled it with Amelia's spicy home-brew which the sweating smith, holding the lid with two hands, drank down swiftly, followed by another helping before William served the smith's father and then the goat-voiced, parchment-skinned carpenter whose pointed Adam's apple bobbed up and down in his brown wasted throat like a bead on an abacus.

There was help and to spare in the hayfield that evening, including collarless Schoolin and Isaiah, both happily reinvesting in the smells and sounds and skills of farm boyhoods. Their waggon, carrying the loader, was drawn to the leeward of the rows, and Schoolin and Isaiah walked side by side with their pitch forks lifting together. From time to time the load-maker called for the ladder and came off his odorous mountain to stand behind the waggon and ensure sides and ends were vertical. The cry 'hold fast' rose from Schoolin or Isaiah as one of them led the horse forward to the next collection point. (It was the omission of the shouted 'hold fast' warning, coupled with the use of a mare with a particularly fast getaway, which led to the death of Cyril, Jimmy the Mole King's brother.)

Then the hay was roped down, a slight bias to the left rectified by differential tightening, and the load was taken to the rising rick. William undertook this job, building a long rectangle on foundations of brushwood and hedge trash. He was always ready to try out new ideas and, the following year, introduced the first haysweep into the parish, a crude but ingenious device, comprising a wooden beam with spikes sticking out before and behind, and horse-drawn by means of two wires. As the sweep moved forward, the spikes slid beneath the hay and when the sweep was fully loaded and had reached the rick, the handle was lifted, the spikes bit and dug into the ground and the load was somersaulted, leaving the pile of hay at the rick, with the sweep moving forward without pause, for the next collection.

Five years later, William introduced the first hay elevator into the parish. It was another thirty years before the first pickup baler appeared in the St Nicholas fields, time for three juvenile generations to lug the cans of potent home-brew to thirsty workers (and take clandestine breath-stopping, head-spinning bravado draughts themselves), to dive and swim, lie and laze, and bury each other alive under the warm rustling waves of cured grass, which stayed in hair and mouths and ears and shoes and shirts, while the redolent dusts and pollens penetrated deep inside juvenile noses, so that they fell asleep as soon as heads touched pillows, still breathing the aromatic nosegays of the curing meadow.

When the Spring Gardens' hay was broached, it had settled tight as the pages of a closed family Bible, redolent and rich as rum-soaked tobacco flake. It was crunchingly sliced from the rick with the big-bladed, razor-sharp carver, straight on one side and curved the other, with a crosspiece handle of polished ash fitted on the cranked iron. William carried the hay in flaps on his head and when he shook it into the mangers, the scent of herbs and legumes and pressed flowers showered through the byre and brought the light of summer to the liquid eyes of his Shorthorns. Lusting tongues curled round the ambrosia and turned the shed into a banquet and the taste the second time round was, to judge from the expression of slit-eyes fulfilment, even better than the first.

This meadow hay was reserved for the dairy, for it was 'always full of milk', and the outlying stock were wintered on grass conserved from coarser pastures. All the milk, except what was sold liquid in the village (which was mostly skim at a penny a pint, anyway) was made into butter in the chill gloaming of the little dairy. This was a half-world between cream and butter, with the brass-bound churn, perforated cream skimmers, scrubbed wooden table, benches and tubs, the mantling ponds of cream in huge shallow bowls, all dully agleam in the northern light, the air laced with the flavour of souring cream, and a tang of sulphur. The thick

stone walls obliterated outside sounds and added to the atmosphere of a temple of which Miss Davis was resident priestess, skimming each evening the cream layers off the milk pans and storing it in shiny enamel pails with a tiny pinch of saltpetre added.

On butter-making day, which was always Saturday, the silent shrine became the noisy butter factory. The churn was dragged from the corner into the centre of the dairy, there was a clatter of buckets and pans and on the occasions when Llewelyn was allowed to be present, William had a pleasant habit of accompanying the event with a little running commentary to explain the mysteries.

'Now then, Llewelyn, we'll just warm up the churn a bit, isn't it,' and the lid of the brass-bound, yellow-grained Pembrokeshire churn bought, like all West Wales churns, from 'Llewhellin the Churn' in Haverfordwest, was unscrewed and removed, and a bucket of steaming water poured in and then drained. William picked up the first of the three precious enamel buckets of cream and the sluggish sour stream fell almost silently among the leaves and planes and paddles of the warmed container. He screwed the lid down tight.

'Now then,' he said, 'get hold by here and then we'll start,' and with his stick arms contributing little or nothing to the motive force beyond pride and eagerness, Llewelyn's arm was taken round and round with the rhythm of William's powerful arm. Half way through, Miss Davis looked in for a few minutes of ritual turning.

The butter 'came' in about half an hour. Half an hour was right. If it came sooner, it was too soft for Miss Davis to form into the firm one-pound rectangular shapes which she fashioned deftly

with her wooden beating pats, imprinting them with the picture of
a buttercuppy mead and a cow grazing – artist's licence this,
for cows will almost sooner die rather than eat those golden
blistering flowers. When the cream was awkward, the butter might
take an hour to come, and temper and energy wore thin, though
there could be no pause or respite except to let the air out through
the peg vent, in order to prevent the churn from frothing, which
was fatal. So the churner just had to go on and on. But mostly a
rhythmical sound – bump-bump-bump, bumpety-bump-bumpety
bumpety – indicated the butter had safely come in the half hour.

William opened the churn and moved to the bench for a
receptacle and, for a moment, Llewelyn put his face close to the
opening and inhaled the acrid freshness of the interior where the
butter showed like golden rocks in the buttermilk ocean. William
undid the plug and the gold-spotted liquid sped into the frothing

crock – a favourite village drink with minty new potatoes, home-baked bread and butter. Then the churn was half-filled with icy cold well water and William began to push together the golden lumps and take out the still streaming wedges with his red, well-scrubbed hands, to pile it carefully in the final washing crock.

Churning was, with the rare exception of the butter refusing to come, an undramatic though an exciting and even faintly magical routine. But one butter-making session was made briefly memorable following the appearance of an unexpected visitor.

Apart from having the licensed parish bull, William Davis kept a billy goat which ran loose with the cows because he believed that the presence of a male goat with the herd was a sovereign safeguard against contagious abortion, the dreaded scourge of the parish dairy farmers. He was a huge stinking animal with magnificently patriarchal head and he marched in and out with the herd from the grazing fields, remaining in the yard while milking was in progress. He served all the nannies in the parish and had a posh pedigree name indicative of aristocratic connections, but was known in the village as 'The Old Nick'.

The churning had gone well this particular Saturday, and now the dairy was peaceful, butter stacked in the wooden crock waiting for Miss Davis to do her moulding and patting, when the door of the dairy which led into the yard was noisily unlatched and the Reverend Isaiah appeared unexpectedly in the opening, holding a large can. He was recognisable as a vicar only by his round clerical hat and a vague aura of blackness, for he was without his collar and had clearly been working in his garden. His face was streaked with sweat, and he had a day's growth of beard.

'Ah, Mr Davis,' he began, 'glad I caught you, glad I caught you . . . hm . . . hm . . . very good . . . very good . . . and Llewelyn too . . . helping no doubt . . . I wondered whether you would be good enough to let me have a little buttermilk to quench my thirst. Dry as a bone . . . would be very grateful.'

He came into the dairy showering his words and exclamations around and pulled the lid from the can with a loud plop, but as he presented the can for the buttermilk, a strange influence spread through the dairy, ousting the familiar sweet/sour sulphur-tinged freshness of the churning day smells. Isaiah had pulled the door to, but left it unlatched and The Old Nick, whose tethered chain had not been properly hasped, was standing in the doorway, shaggy and huge, filling the cold confines with the acrid salty reek of billy

goat. As the pungent cloud reached Isaiah, he turned in surprise
and then said brightly, 'Ah, good boy, good boy . . . must be
smelling my nannies . . . there . . . good lad, good lad . . .' and
advanced to close the door.

William Davis acted like a man who saw the situation differently,
'Look out,' he shouted and picking the crock of freshly-made
butter, carried it quickly to the stonebench on the wall.

Isaiah continued to flatter and appease with his stream of
'good boy, good boy . . . hm . . . hm . . .'

'Baa' said the billy, lowered his head and charged. Isaiah
dropped his can and sought escape on the unlocked churn which
began to revolve and, as he fell, the billy caught him in the seat.
He rose and staggered forward, and came to rest with one arm
in the butter crock. Cowering and frightened, Llewelyn climbed
on to the table. As the dairy reverberated to the thunderous blows
of an empty cream pan on the head of The Old Nick, by dint
of continuous belabouring, William drove the trespasser from the

dairy and back into the yard, past a shrinking pale-faced Miss
Davis, who had remembered with fear the prophecy of the local
'Millions Now Living Will Never Die' representative from
Fishguard, who only the previous evening had prophesied
impending doom for the world, on the village green. That was the
first and last appearance of the billy goat anywhere near the
Spring Gardens dairy, for after that, while the cows remained out
of doors, he wore a tethering chain with a new hasp attached
which rattled and tinkled as he marched with the cows through
the village, and was used to tie him up safely while summer
milking and, especially, summer churning, were in progress.

In summer – just as in winter he climbed the stairs to the solitude
of the attic – Schoolin's son would escape from the gang to the
lonely fields and dingles round the village. Favourite haunt was
the Well Meadow – alive with armies of bumble bees probing the
corollas and rocking the long-stalked clovers as they zoomed off
with brimming saddlebags – where the bank above the little
stream was redolent with willowherb and meadowsweet.

Llewelyn's destination this summer morning was the wild
watercress bed where nibbling crisp peppery stalks and leaves
furnished an added inducement to linger and dream.

Llewelyn climbed over the gate, and then stopped. A strange
girl was squatting in the well stream and, uncertain as always, of
confronting a stranger, especially a girl, he began to whistle loudly,
kicking with a show of bravado at the young reeds growing in the
damp approaches to the bed. He stopped ten yards away down-
stream and looked furtively at the squatting barefoot figure.
She was small, with a tangled mass of black curls falling over her

eyes, the skin of her faintly foreign face dark, almost swarthy, her tiny mouth, perfect as a pimpernel flower. Llewelyn recognised her. She had called at his father's back door the previous evening when Nana bought two dozen clothes pegs of gleaming willow from her gypsy mother.

She stood up and faced him with a quick movement of her body, her dress clutched in both hands above her waist. Llewelyn's heart began to beat fast, his stare riveted on the mysteriously bare triangle above her slightly opened brown thighs. She looked at him, the expression in her black gypsy eyes wise and confident, conscious of her power over the little *goy* with the heart-shaped face and big grey eyes she had seen and liked the night before.

Not far from panic flight now, Llewelyn sought help, as he always did in moments of crisis, from the big words, always faithfully waiting and ready with their power and glory, to help banish his shrinking fears. Small forefinger out-stretched from a tight fist, pulses hammering, he pointed at her thighs, and said in a gruff breathless voice, 'I think there is something medically unusual there.'

Transferring her dress to one hand, and touching herself lightly, instinctively understanding the purport of the strange words, she replied with a toss of her curls, 'No, there aint. I'm a proper lady. I'm Mary Rose.'

A confusion of images, of foals and mares and lambs and ewes and ducks and drakes – that passed their family lives under the school banks – of pigeons that rode each other pick-a-back in Schoolin's yard in the spring, jostled in his mind with the half-understood explanations of the facts of life from the shopkeeper's nephew, and as though drawn by invisible threads hooked into his

blood, he began to walk towards her through the watercress. The
water rose over his boots, and poured into his socks, but this
usually world-eclipsing event hardly registered anymore.

They met without a word and stood together, their foreheads
touching like a pair of calves, breathing each other's warm breath,
hers faintly tinted with the green juice of chewed watercress. And
words and phrases and images from the novelettes about
aristocrats and village beauties, whose lives and loves unfolded
through the winter evenings in the guttering gold of Nana's
kitchen candlelight, jumbled in his mind.

The love affair had lasted less than a minute when a huge voice
erupted from the far end of the field, and with a gasped 'It's my
father', Mary Rose's bare brown legs twinkled through the
buttercups in frightened obedience in the direction of the roar.
That afternoon, the gipsy's piebald mare, hitched into the shafts
of the kingfisher caravan, the foal trotting alongside and the tied
dogs running behind, passed briskly through the village, and
Mary Rose vanished for ever.

The summer had been kind to Moonlight the Shire foal.
Throughout the hot days, between play and sleep, he had drawn
from the mare's rich sugary fountain, up to five gallons of milk on
some days, though always ready to bunt and bully his mother's
long-suffering udder with his greedy muzzle for more. For two
whole months, excused from all heavy work, the mare had grazed
around him in circumferences of care, his silhouette constant in
the mirrors of her eyes, while her metronome munch and drag of
massive hooves through toppling scented clover were his unfailing
lullabies. His body, especially his legs, grew and strengthened with
unbelievable rapidity and, now in his fourth month, he was already
walking by his mother's side as she worked in the fields, loosely
attached to her harness. When the mare worked in trace, he

F

waited, usually with a companion, in the well-fenced paddock near the house, where he learnt to eat hay and crushed oats, and become an accomplished grazer.

As the summer came to an end, and the dark-green mangold leaves met across the rows, and the fields of Little Joss wheat were tinged with nine-carat gold, the milk hairs on the foal's neck and legs loosened and fell away.

On one afternoon, he lay fast asleep, stretched out on the warm earth, motionless from mottled velvet muzzle to black hearth-brush tail, legs rocking-horse wide, blissfully unaware that weaning time was here. A lilt of breeze ruffled his mane, wafted thistledown on to his blaze. He slept on. A speeding dragonfly jerked him half-couchant, ears semaphoring amazement, pool-pupils sun-glazed. The dragonfly returned, cutting through the paddock like a power-saw. Muscles bunched, he soared to his feet with astonishing power and grace, ready to greet his mother with scampering whinnying delight. But she was not there, and did not return that evening or any other, until mother's milk was forgotten and true adulthood had begun.

CHAPTER TWELVE

Cries of Autumn

*'Thirty years ago in Pembrokeshire a 300-acre farm would yield
the tenant or owner-occupier a hundred pounds a year as his share
of the annual rabbit harvest . . .'*

Country Life, 12 August 1954.

The 300-acre farm referred to here is Tresissillt, which is a mile
from St Nicholas village. In 1924 over 5000 wild rabbits were
trapped and sold from this farm alone. Yet at the beginning of the
century, the rabbits on this sea-bounded holding had numbered
so few that they were given as an annual perquisite to a farm hand
in exchange for his services in killing the pig.

The proliferation of the few into a major pest had its origin in
two happenings that hit the parish more or less at the same time,
the arrival of the iron gin-trap and the economic depression
which began to decimate the farming industry. Within five years
of the arrival of the gin in the parish, the rabbits had become a
major industry, a source of substantial profit for dealers like
Bilbow, a lifeline for the low-output farms teetering on the verge
of bankruptcy, and a livelihood for numerous trappers. The rabbits
were 'farmed' in an unholy partnership between the farmer and the
freelance trapper who received an agreed percentage of the season's
takings, and made sure he left enough does untrapped to produce
next year's crop.

Bilbow bought all the parish rabbits and railed them daily from Goodwick station to the Welsh mining valleys.

The imminence of the season was signalled for Schoolin's household when neighbour Dafydd Moon began to oil his gins, adjusted so the slightest pressure on the plates brought serrated jaws together with a vicious snap of iron. Dafydd Moon and the other trappers were mild men, but from October onwards their trade spread a crepuscular blight through the fields where they operated. As the October dusk deepened, rabbits making the jump from burrows to begin feeding landed on the cunningly sited gins, the iron jaws snapped shut and the screaming began.

Many hunting cats from the village shared the rabbits' fate and were never seen again unless the trapper, recognising the animal as belonging to a particular household, took the trouble to set it free – but a quick truncheon blow was a less troublesome way of solving the problem. The gins killed the rabbits' predators and the pheasants and partridges, and thinned the ranks of the Pembrokeshire buzzards. A trapped buzzard, earthbound and disgraced, flapping his great wings in an abortive effort to return to his boundless kingdom was a tragic sight.

Schoolin's son was closely involved with the commerce because of his friendship with Bilbow's nephew, and accompanied Jack on his rounds in the high-sided trap – loaded with empty dark-brown wicker hampers, each with two stout internal cross-members on which to hang the night's catch – clinging to his big companion as they clattered out of the village, down the empty, narrow roads.

First call was Tresissillt Farm where Dafydd Moon had degutted sixty couples and hung them in twos with spliced back legs in the shadowy barn. The paunched harvest of the night hung rigid, eyes bulging and glazed, lips peeled back over teeth, broken leg bones showing through the skin where they had struggled in the iron jaws: comestibles not creatures any more, making no demands on heart and pity.

Llewelyn worked hard, helping pack them away, dimly conscious of the smell of fur and dried blood which stayed in his fingernails and nostrils all day. Then they drove away along a mile of level lane, past hedgerows dripping with sloes and hawthorn berries and wreathed with traveller's joy on which the late autumn sun laid a patina of gold; down the steep hill where the mare's hunched, braking cruppers were assisted by grating wooden brake blocks on the iron-banded wheels, along the ferny trail where the streams and rivulets from a dozen parishes joined and chattered through saplings and undergrowth on their way to the sea. As they passed the garden of a derelict cottage, Jack was able to pull down some branches of 'Ladies Fingers', juicy and sour but free.

Six couples only at Old Mill, then back along the lane to New Mill – a name which told the story of why the remotely sited Old Mill had declined. The widowed owner's son, a limping consumptive of fifteen, left leg bones shortened by bovine tuberculosis, hectic cheeks pale with flour dust, closed the half-door of the mill to mute the clatter.

'What's this then?' he asked, affecting surprise. 'Schoolin's son going in for the rabbits then, is it?' He looked at Jack, 'Only five pair,' and added, 'hardly worth calling for, is it?'

Then it was downhill and across the ford of the river which had once turned a dozen wheels on its way from St Nicholas to the sea, and on to the most important waterwheel in the parish, where the trapped rabbits and smallholding were ancillary to the main task, which was making cloth from the unwashed fleeces of Welsh ewes.

All the processes were undertaken on site, even to the dyeing of the cloth which was displayed in rolls for sale in the fleece-redolent parlour of the house. The owner was a quiet man with glistening curls who perhaps had learned to hoard his words in a world where silence was the sound of falling water. He exuded quiet authority but on this morning was uncharacteristically engaged in altercation with a short-statured woman dressed in an oilskin, calf-length laced boots and an old trilby hat.

She spoke in querulous, half-accusing tones, 'Only two blankets you say, Mr Griffiths? Surprised Gwilym will be that the fleeces only made two, isn't it?'

'Surprised he shouldn't be, Mrs Morgan,' came the quiet firm rejoinder, 'for every scrap of wool we could save from your fleeces has gone into those blankets'. His expression grew stern as he added, 'Nobody gets cheated at this mill, you know.'

'No, no, Mr Griffiths, not saying that I am at all,' came the quick reply. 'Just that Gwilym will be disappointed, that's all. You know how it is.'

Llewelyn moved away while Jack loaded the rabbits, and stared over a half-door into the roaring world of wool and water where Eli, the six-and-a-half-feet tall, hired weaver – who walked home a total return journey of thirty miles to Maenclochog in the Prescelly Mountains each weekend – was minding the machines. He was a poet of prize-winning repute in the local Eisteddfod, and was often seen on summer evenings, away from the oily roar of his machines – where he declaimed verse and sang all day – staring at the sea in Abermawr, seeking perhaps a bardic-weaver's inspiration from the clashing loom of the tide.

After three more calls, the final collection at Trefelgarn Farm brought the daily total to two hundred couples, and was followed by a frantic rush to catch the rabbit train to Cardiff. The older Jack, already a personality of panache and enormous strength – he could lift 56-lb weights above his head at sixteen years of age – was Llewelyn's hero.

Night fell before their return and the boys drove home in darkness, candle-lamps casting feeble gleams, foxes barking, owls goody-hooing eerily in the dingles, bats swooping within inches of their hair, to arrive in time for a late tea. Then they helped Aunt Aggie in the low-roofed milking hovel where the legs of the milking stool sank and settled lower and lower into the earthen floor, and the air smelled of green cow flop, garlicky emanations of breath and cud and rankly steaming bodies.

Llewelyn milked Molly, a pacific bony matron of charming
temperament and small manure-grimed easily encompassed
Ayrshire teats which, on Mrs Bilbow's instructions, he kept
lubricated with liberal applications of froth from the bucket. For
his contribution to the evening's toil, he was allowed to drink as
many cupfuls of milk as he could hold, taken straight and uncooled
and delicious from the profusely yielding warm hairy udder. The
brindled, crumple-horned Molly calved like clockwork every
October, and never seemed to be dry.

Away from the rabbit-infested fields, the cooler days of late
autumn brought the parish pig-sticker to the village for his annual
round of duty. The pig was not a luxury all could afford. The
Squire, rector, schoolmaster, shopkeeper, William Davis of Spring
Gardens and the smallholders had their own. The rest of the
village, except for the poverty-stricken tailor and schoolcleaner,
shared co-operatively the cost of fattening a pig, though quarrels
about costs and returns could break up the agreement.

Pig killing was doubly the most public event in the village
calendar, firstly because it was a matter of material concern to
those who were on the give-and-take list for bits and pieces of
pork and innards and, secondly, because the event was stridently
advertised by the dying screams which shrilled through the
customary Saturday morning stillness.

Schoolin bought his pig (sometimes two) in the spring. The sty
inmate was sometimes a hog, sometimes a sow, but whatever the
sex or lack of it, the simple aim was to grow and fatten the tenant
to gargantuan proportions until literally he or she could hardly

walk. Just as geese were expected to provide both meat and golden grease for cooking (and rubbing in to cure chest complaints), so the pig was expected to stock the kitchen beams with bacon and ham and the pantry shelves with serried ranks of earthenware jars filled to the brim with snow-white lard as well.

Of the tenants of the schoolmaster's sty over the years, none converted barley meal, potatoes, cabbage leaves, household scraps and cinder nuggets into more pink pork, bacon and white lard, or more intimately engaged the affections of her owners in the process than Blodwen the sow, who, in the opinion of the farmer who helped bring her into the world and then took her out of it, weighed at least 400lb on the death bench. She was always remembered for the fright she once gave the family, and by Llewelyn for a truly traumatic execution.

Blodwen was crossbred from a white pedigree Welsh boar on a black and white Saddleback sow, which married an aristocratic lean-meat father with a dam who ran to fat like the traditional lady at the fair and thus combined the best of both worlds. There developed between the Joneses and Blodwen a relationship of exceptional affection and trust though it is doubtful if Blodwen ever saw her human attendants for, like her mother, her ears were the size of rhubarb leaves and covered her face like curtains which ensured her line of vision was restricted to the over-riding priority of the food under her nose, though she undoubtedly recognised her various servitors by voice, and responded accordingly.

She was a model tenant, kept herself and her bedroom as clean as Nana's kitchen, ridding herself of the wastes, which Schoolin

fed to his insatiable garden, with modesty and regularity in her outside toilet – that is, until the Saturday morning when Nana came down the steps into the kitchen with the pregnant words, 'There's something the matter with Blodwen. She won't get up and she's left nearly all her food.' Then with her penchant for melodrama and seeing the lurid possibilities of any situation, Nana added, 'Wouldn't it be terrible if Blodwen died?'

There was a stunned silence and, conscious of the expression of bereavement on Nana's face, the grandmother leaned forward and asked no one in particular, 'What did Nana say? Did she say that poor Miss Morgan is dead at last? Poor dab, but it'll be a relief too . . .' she added, seeking a bright side to the passing of the hunchback seamstress.

In a voice that contained more than a hint of impatience, Nana called across, 'It's nothing to do with Ruth Morgan, it's *Blodwen*. She's not well. We think she may be very ill – and she has still got six weeks to go . . .'

The old lady lifted her hands in dismay and the gravity of her expression deepened.

Meanwhile Schoolin was at the sty. Blodwen lay, head on front legs, breathing stertorously, making no response to exhortation, to gentle rump slapping, not even to the rattle of the food bucket which always brought her off her bracken couch.

Schoolin said, 'I think she's got a stoppage. We'll need John Evans to get her drenched.'

Any sign that a pig was not doing its superporcine utmost to eat itself to glory with maximum despatch earned a drench of Epsoms Salts and senna tea. But the supine Blodwen showed no improvement, nor did milk and buttermilk, gruel and Welsh broth do anything to bring her from the grim threshold where her snout rested. For the first time ever, there loomed the possibility that a four-fifths grown pig would have to be stuck in her own dining-room to avoid dying a natural death. The news spread through the village.

It was Dafydd Moon, the rabbit trapper, who saved Blodwen. On his advice he and Schoolin hurried to Aberbach, armed with hammers and chisels, scrambled over kelp-covered rocks and harvested two half sackfuls of limpets and mussels. The shellfish were boiled in Dafydd's furnace pan, filling the village with a fume of ocean.

The reeking posset, with bits of limpet and mussel floating on top, was poured into Blodwen's trough and dragged under her nose. There were ten people present to confirm the miracle. For perhaps two minutes the strong vapours curling round her snout produced no results. Then moved by who knows what atavistic memory, a tiny left ear movement was discernible, the faintest of grunts audible, the left ear lifted another fraction and then, with infinite slowness, Blodwen lifted her huge-jowled head and let it hang for a moment over the crustacean caudle. A moment later came the blessed sound of 'slop slop' and Schoolin spoke the emotion and relief of all when he said, 'There's a good one, there's my old beauty, there's my beauty,' and he slapped little, grinning Dafydd Moon on his shoulder so it was not clear who was being eulogised.

A few minutes later Blodwen rose, wobbled and wavered, and repaired to the corner where she spent the next ten minutes laboriously producing goodies for Schoolin's garden.

Llewelyn's mother looked affectionately at the little trapper. 'We must make sure Mrs Moon gets a really nice piece of pork, a really nice piece,' she said with a brilliant smile.

Alas, Blodwen's return to health and beauty was short-lived, for six weeks later Llewelyn leaned over the sty to rub her back and take her mind off the breakfast which was never to arrive. From the age of eight when he first watched with horrified fascination to the time he went to Fishguard County School at twelve, he never failed to shed tears at the impending fate of these trusting friends that the family came to love, but was fatally drawn to the execution.

A shadow fell over the sty and Mr Williams, the mild, slow-moving, tooth-sucking, pig-sticker, wearing a leather apron and carrying a rope, stood at his side. He cast an appreciative eye over Blodwen's pink contours and spoke in crooning tones as he unlatched the door.

'Well, Blodwen, you are an old beauty and no joking. There

now, just look what I've got . . .' he said, rubbing her head with
the Judas friendliness of the executioner about to ply his trade, so
that Blodwen opened her mouth in trusting appreciation. With
lightening speed he imprisoned her top jaw with a running noose,
pressed her against the wall and pulled the rope tight. Accustomed
to love and friendship and treats and back-scratching from humans,
Blodwen screamed in terrified protest as with huge strength and
long expertise, aided by the pushing Schoolin and Dafydd Moon,
Mr Williams manhandled the sow through the door and brought
her to the place of death under the tree. The rope was thrown
over a branch of the ash.

Suddenly Llewelyn, his heart throbbing like a humming bird's
wings, decided to run away but was too late for he was commanded to
'hold her tail' by the butcher. From his carpenter's frail, the big
man took out his long thin killing knife, honed to a sliver. He knelt
down and felt for the right spot with his left hand and with
visible effort pushed the knife through the tough skin and bristle
into the sow's throat. He missed the artery, withdrew it and had
to cut in again, and this time with a hacking motion as though
cutting a piece of tough cloth, until a sudden rush of blood
indicated the jugular had been severed – as did Blodwen's curdling
screams.

Unexpectedly she lurched backwards, the rope slackened, the
noose slipped off her jaw and she staggered screaming and bleeding
down the yard with Llewelyn alone hanging on to her tail. In
terror he heard the butcher's roar '*pull down*, pull down on her

tail' and he did with all his young might and in some way this upset the weakening Blodwen's balance and she fell over, and with the butcher and helpers quickly on the scene and kneeling on her side, she finally bled her life away with a last whimper into the ground.

Llewelyn began to weep and was comforted by Schoolin. The Dead March from 'Saul' was being belted out *fortissimo* by his mother on the dining-room piano in an attempt to drown the dying screams echoing in the yard, for the screams from her future bacon supplies affected her deeply.

But in a few minutes, with Blodwen on the bench and Dafydd Moon arriving with buckets of boiling water, Llewelyn had forgotten the beastliness. The rank smell of scalding loosened bristle filled the air as Mr Williams carved long, de-bristling swathes with his curry comb, dunked and shaved the curtaining hair round the ears with barber care, removed white eyebrows from above little sunken piggy eyes which had hardly been seen in life, and deftly flayed the trotters. Then the butcher broke the front legs so they hung limp and compounded the finality of her ending. With huge effort, a few feet at a time, the bench loaded with a gleaming white thing which bore no relationship to life and love and Blodwen, the death gash in the throat faded now to an inoffensive dog-rose pink, was taken down the steps and through the kitchen. With a series of rhythmical 'Now all together, one two three' commands from the butcher, the harvest of the sty was hoisted foot by grinding foot into the back-kitchen ceiling beams, where it was lashed by the Achilles sinews, spread-eagled on a round gambrel of ash.

Nana appeared in the doorway. 'What do you think of her then, Mr Williams,' she asked with an excited smile.

The butcher sucked his teeth and signalled the carcase as he replied, 'I reckon all of twenty score. Biggest you've ever had. Certainly the biggest I've ever killed for you.'

Nana relayed the news to the grandmother in a loud excited voice. 'Fancy that! Mr Williams puts Blodwen at twenty score. The biggest pig we've ever killed. There's good, isn't it?'

The ancient raised her hands in astonishment, approval and gratitude.

'A real Acraman pig . . .' Nana said, giving Blodwen the ultimate family accolade.

With noisy fluency, the butcher honed a new knife, bigger and wider than the dagger-pointed killing blade, revolved the carcase on its creaking gambrel to catch the northern light, and drew the shining blade with careful precision between the two-seven-a-side lines of small virgin teats, until the pink guideline joined the gash in the throat. Then he cut in deeply, the walls of fat parted and opened, the voluptuous reek of hot insides and vital fluids flooded the kitchen. He cut away the moorings and with effort lifted the squelching mass of streaming blue-grey gut into the galvanised bath.

Goodies were salvaged and segregated – brown kidneys, dark blood-frothed liver were placed in Nana's enamel dish, the big pluck of lights put by to boil for the Indian Game cockerels, the bladder, expertly excised, squeezed and emptied – a process which always produced a grin from the butcher – and passed to Llewelyn. Later, Schoolin would fill the tough bag with straining breath, tie it with a leather lace and hang it in the beams to dry, until it cured into a virtually punctureless winter football. Finally,

the carcase was sluiced down with cold well water, a potato inserted to keep the mouth open and the door carefully secured against Boof and Butterpaws.

Schoolin and family went to bed agog with harvest excitement, nourished by back-kitchen visits, to bathe the carcase in the gold light of high-held candles, regaling themselves with the glory of the fulfilled and forgotten Blodwen. Ten o'clock the following day the butcher arrived, with his frail of cutting-up instruments. Pig was held motionless by Schoolin and Dafydd Moon as he cut off the head, carved through the tendons to remove the front feet, halved the carcase with short, sharp, cunningly-timed blows with his black-bladed butcher chopper and laid the two halves of the pig on the cold blue stone slab which ran the length of one wall. He measured, cut off, shaped, trimmed and tidied the hams, sides and shoulders. A piece from the backbone fillet was cut out for his own lunch which, when his task was finished, filled the kitchen with the nasal manna of fried fresh-killed pork.

The butcher mounted his bike, pedalled away with five shillings and a joint, and the family moved into the back kitchen to allocate pieces to those on the take-and-give list, especially on this occasion to Mrs Moon.

Using salt from the two 7-lb salt loaves, crunchingly flattened with the rolling pin, and heaped high in readiness from the previous night, Nana began to rub pink flesh and snow-white fat with seven of salt to one of saltpetre mixture. The hams were later treated with brown sugar, and remained a week longer than the flitches and shoulders which were lifted, washed, drained, dried, and hung from the blacksmith's rafter hooks after three weeks. (Curing was always a success except for one shameful year when a ham cut after four months in the rafters was found to be maggoty and, taken out after dark, given a felon's burial in the midden.) The head was boiled to make jellied brawn.

In the evening, chopped liver, pork scraps, heart, onions, leaves of dried sage and fresh parsley, were mixed with stale breadcrumbs in a deep-dish by Llewelyn's grandmother, who signified her completion, as she had for twenty years (as though accepting a novitiate), with the words 'bring on the veil', and the lacy membrane of lard which had enclosed Blodwen's stomach was cut into little squares. The old lady laboriously rolled helpings of the mixture into small balls in the hollow of her palm, encasing the savoury bombs with cut-up sections of the veil. Finally she cleaned the mix off her fingers, laid the faggots side by side in the baking dishes, sucked her wedding ring and for the next fireside hour regaled her ancient nose with the rich fumes of her faggots which filled the kitchen with cargoes of fragrance, the memory of which gives Llewelyn jaw-ache after fifty years.

Finally, when the body fat had been cut into squares, it was heated slowly in a big iron saucepan, kept well-stirred for up to two hours as the last of Blodwen disappeared in a sea of simmering liquor, and lightly salted, drained, and white as a lily of the valley, was poured into the fawn and brown-collared earthenware jars, identical with those which held the yellow goose-grease which was rubbed into the chest against bronchial conditions.

Although Schoolin's salary never quite tipped £6 a week, the family ate (and drank) sumptuously throughout their life in the village, and his wife Catherine saved over £3000 as well. They bought the minimum of food. Schoolin's garden was a cornucopia, vegetables a dish in their own flavourful right and, apart from the mountainous pig, Schoolin filled the larder by his gun and rod. The Plymouth Rock hens produced eggs for the house, and for sale to the Fowlman who circulated the district in a pensioned-off solid-tyred red Trojan van, used for twenty previous years as a Brooke Bond tea van, and was the most familiar motor in the Welsh countryside of those days. The Fowlman bought eggs and culled cocks and hens as necessary. Schoolin's hens were mated to lusty, meaty, dawn-celebrating Indian Game cockerels, to produce Sunday roast fowls whose necks were stretched each Saturday morning by the schoolmaster with an elegant absence of fuss and pain and sorrow.

The larder was filled with wild and garden jams, jellies and chutneys, and mountains of hazel nuts were harvested. Each year, too, masses of spicy, cowslip flowers and primroses – six parts primroses to two of cowslip – infused with boiled well water, laced with honey, ginger and cloves, and allowed to honeymoon together in the vat for three days, permeated the house with the essences of fields and hedgerows, so that the walls ran rivulets of fragrance. The added yeast turned the mantling infusion into a chuckling must and, when this had died down, Schoolin poured in a bottle of brandy before filling the little cask with the wine, where the wild nectar matured a whole year before broaching.

From the cromlech, the unfolding parish panorama changed little with the cries of autumn. The image remained, principally stone and rock and sea. A few fields of stooked corn interpolated a touch of husbandry into the wildness here and there, but cereal-growing in the parish was limited, for the depredations of the ubiquitous rabbit were a constant disincentive except to the most determined husbandman and there were not many of these apart from a few of those with the bigger acreages. In the farm fields, the principal change was embodied in the lighter emerald greens of the latter-math, following late haymaking, while a few fields of green rape for autumn and winter grazing added sporadic shades of a deeper hue.

It was in the close-up roadside hedgerow-banks of St Nicholas that one found the true colour of autumn. These equilateral ramparts, up to eight foot high, were built on a heavy stone base, using the distinctive long-handled Welsh shovels which look graceless and clumsy to the uninitiated but which, like the scythe, became tools of grace and strength in the hands of the St Nicholas roadmen. The earthen heart of the bank was built with material dug from the adjoining field headlands, faced on the outside with thick turves, built up in courses, with each course 'broken' on to the course below, the grass side facing outwards, and terminating in a parapet of earth planted with gorse and hawthorn. In a short time, from the wild seeds lying dormant in the headland soil, and from seeds carried in by winds and birds and small mammals, the fantastic riches of these great wild fruit and flower gardens began to riot and blaze.

The hedgerow harvest had its inevitable effect on school punctuality, for most of the children loitered in the lush lanes and had to rush to try and beat the school bell, but somebody was sure to lose a mark every day throughout September, arriving in school with tell-tale blackberry stains on the teeth, or with a pocket full of sloes, or nuts or haws. But of the items most responsible for late arrival at school, swedes were the principal culprits and the stone-hard juicy yellow flesh from the small purple globes stolen on the way to school by the bigger boys was the staple dinner-time supplement of the back end of every year.

Autumn brought wild mushrooms in a profusion unknown on horseless farms of today, especially in the permanent pastures, some of them unploughed for a hundred years.

Seven o'clock one autumn Saturday morning found Schoolin and his son walking up the rise to Trefelgarn Farm. Sea, sky, the

granite eminence of Samson's Quoit, even the berried hedgerows a few yards away were shrouded in morning mist. Only footsteps and breathing broke the silence. The ball of the sun played hide and seek, rolling in and out like some tantalising target at a fair and Schoolin, always eager beaver to arrive at his destination when on the trail of loot, walked fast until they reached the gate, hung on massive stone pillars.

'Let's start from the hedge, Llewelyn,' he half whispered, obeying the cautious instinct of years of dubious harvesting with his clerical mate, Isaiah, 'and we'll go up the field a few yards apart. In that way we won't miss any. I don't think there are any rabbit traps here yet.'

He pointed to a heap of horse manure and said, again in a whisper as though determined not to warn the bailiff, or at least, not spread the good news, 'That's the sign, Llewelyn, plenty of horse dung means plenty of mushrooms. Always. Always.'

His lips parted, stubbly cheeks creased in a smile of anticipation as he and his son moved apart into the heavy mist and disappeared from each other. Almost immediately, the earth began to teem with fruit as the old field lived up to its name of the Mushroom Field. Here . . . here . . . here . . . Llewelyn's grubby little fingers darted and plucked, darted and plucked. It was like the time he found three half crowns on the road, a bonanza with which he nearly bought up all the peardrops in Bilbow's shop.

Then he stumbled across the site of an old rick base rotted into compost, as rich as one of his grandmother's faggots, and suddenly a mushroom, the size of a saucer at least, glowed at his feet, surrounded by a whole dinner set of treasure trove.

'Dad,' he called urgently, 'come over by here quick.'

Unbelievingly he levered out the huge fruit with two fingers, lifted it to his nostrils and inhaled the rich fume of the dark-chocolate fluted undersides. Then he began to worry they were poisonous fungi after all, until his father took it from him with a hoarse chuckling whisper and gesture of joy, as though he had met Mr Pickwick in the mist.

Then without warning, an unexpected eddy blew a hole in the milky morning and, a few yards away, the four farm Shires materialised in a brown statuary of stone. Father and son stood and stared, mushroom bonanza temporarily forgotten, mesmerised by the majesty of the horses. Llewelyn had seen them all some time at the smithy, Old Meg the twenty-year-old brood mare, head hanging low, one resting hoof tilted on edge almost hidden by yellow-stained feather; her daughter, Bronwen, whose back hooves wore those specially heavy bespoke shoes of Meiriog's, to shorten her stride – with her head and shawl mane drooping over her mother's back, a part of the matriarchal stillness: the geldings Jack and Rowly, posed and poised each side of the old mare's head, rooted and motionless.

Suddenly the sun came floating through the cloud and the dull brown quartet was cast in glowing copper, long enough for the scream of gulls flying inland to follow the plough, the echoing call of peewits on an adjacent stubble, one wild cry from a curlew, the plaintive loner of the marshes to be heard.

Then, the sun went out and the statues vanished in the mist.

CHAPTER THIRTEEN

Grannies in the Corner

'*Owing to Mrs Acraman's funeral from the School House,
the school was closed for the day. Permission for the closure
has been obtained from the Assistant Director.*'

Headmaster's Log Book, 21 September 1932

In those days, it seemed there was a grandmother or grandfather
by every parish fireside and inglenook where old people sat and
nodded out the end of their lives. However small the house or
cottage, the notion of throwing out a mother or father (or brother,
sister, aunt, uncle, nephew or niece for that matter) because they
were old or sick or helpless was unimaginable. Admittedly, in
this pre-antibiotic age, old people did not live as long as today and,
in any case, there was no place for them to go except the
workhouse. But old people *were* cherished and respected for what
they had been and had done in the community.

Schoolin gave his mother-in-law a home for over twenty years,
and for Llewelyn especially she remained throughout childhood
a cornerpiece delight, candlewick-shawled, vast-skirted, black-
aproned, white shining hair tightly stretched in a bun that grew

tighter with the years. She had a waxy facial shine which remained unclouded and pink to the end of her days. Ba sat by the fireside oven, booted or slippered feet on a footstool, lap a broad shiny surface, frequently occupied by the cats, though when fruit or other tribute was arriving in season she liked to keep it clear for reception of any goodies that were going.

After the age of six and until he won a scholarship to Fishguard County School and had to leave home, Llewelyn was involved in important private arrangements with her, to keep her supplied with the seasonal produce of Schoolin's garden.

'How are they getting on then? Are there any ready for Ba yet?' The old lady never referred to supplies by name. Llewelyn repaired to the garden to establish that *they* were hardly more than small green pimples with disproportionate tops and tails.

'They're not ready, Ba' he returned with his report, 'but I've brought some for you to see.'

With speed the green pimples were pocketed, except one which was topped and tailed with a dark-ridged thumbnail and popped into her mouth, savoured until any flavour had been extracted when the residue would be consigned to the flames. Ba's proximity to the fire gave her an easy disposal for apple cores, toffee papers, plum stones, biscuit debris, sweet packets, nut shells and other remains of clandestine treats from her lap and pockets.

The bearing of fruits which began with the hard immature green warts off the old goosegog bushes went on throughout most of the year. Red currants were followed by black, by peas, beans, plums, apples, pears. Then the hedgerows came into their own with blackberries, blue-black sloes, tart enough to buckle iron

and just about as yielding, but great favourites because they were fine keepers, and red bunches from the hawthorn trees. The old lady smelled faintly of oranges most of the year because she kept the peel until it was dry and brittle and then put on little firework displays for her grandson, feeding the peel through the firebars where it burned with an effervescing blue flame.

There was also a flow of sweets, especially from a large flower-painted casket of toffee made each week by Nana from sugar, butter, vinegar and essence of lemon, a product of variable flavour, for sometimes Nana's pre-occupation with the cards caused the bubbling confection to be forgotten and end up like black glass with a dark flavour of burning. The toffee container was kept above the fireplace where Ba couldn't get at it. For these ministrations, Llewelyn was paid a Saturday morning wage from Ba's ten shillings weekly old age pension.

Like his son, Schoolin had a close understanding with his mother-in-law. In particular, Ba had a symbiotic relationship with his right arm. He armed her to the garden, church, the school wall – where she could sit and see and smell the sea – the fields when cowslips or blackberries were being picked.

From 1926 Schoolin had a new role when he bought a four-seater car costing £212 (inclusive of side screens). The village turned out to watch its arrival. Neighbour Dafydd Moon, the rabbit trapper and village handyman and mechanic, came into Schoolin's yard, circled it once and then spelled out the make, 'C-L-Y-N-O' . . . not a Morris Cowley then? Why is that, Mr Jones? Good cars the Cowleys.'

Nana took it on herself to reply. 'Mr Jones has bought this car because it is better, Mr Moon. You see, this isn't an ordinary car,' she added, although her understanding of cars was on a par with that of Anne Boleyn or Julius Caesar in their day.

Eventually Ba was togged in her best clothes and armed to the Clyno to 'go for a drive'. She sat by the driver, in high-collared

black dress with glittering sequins, candlewick shawl, large
flower-bowl hat and high polished black lace-up boots, and rode
through the village beaming and waving with royal vagueness on
her way to Abermawr beach where she remained in the car with
'the side screens down', staring and smiling and nodding and
enjoying the sea air.

The Clyno also expanded her social life, for Schoolin was now
able to bring her an occasional visitor from her old days as a girl
in Fishguard. When the lady known as Aunt Evans was brought
along in the Clyno for her visit, their joint ages added up to
170 years. Schoolin armed the ancient visitor over the threshold
into the interior gloom. Llewelyn was mesmerised by Aunt
Evans' hatpin, which was long enough to pierce the heart of a
whale.

Her visitor stared a moment at Ba who was nodding and smiling
and holding out her hand. Then as though she had just realised
why she was there, she addressed Ba with her maiden name,
'Joanna Nicholas, Joanna Nicholas, how are you?' Ba held out her
left hand which her visitor rather severely ignored and took her
deeply veined birdy right one which was afflicted with arthritis.
While his mother and Nana were making tea, Llewelyn was sent
in to offer a choice of shop peardrops or a piece of Nana's home-
made toffee, which on this occasion was under-cooked and
warranted to demoralise denture wearers.

Llewelyn's first intimation of something wrong came when the
visitor leaned forward and said, 'Tell me, Joanna, how is your
husband Ivor then?' He knew that his grandfather Acraman had
died before he was born, but Ba whose worst ear was next to

Aunt Evans had caught the name only and replied with a happy smile about her youngest son.

'Oh, Ivor's done very well indeed. He is Superintendent of the Manchester Ship Canal.'

Puzzled and astonished, Llewelyn heard Aunt Evans continue with a new subject as though Ba had never spoken, 'It's a terrible thing The Drink, all my life I have fought it. Ever since we came back from Chile. We built the Temperance Hall in Fishguard, you know. It was so wonderful, like a sign, when we got a piece of land right next to the chapel at Bethel. Of course the drink ruined Ivor Acraman, you know. Thank God, Catherine took you away in time. It would have ruined you too, Joanna, for you loved the gin. You know that, don't you?'

Llewelyn's eyes were the size of his mother's best saucers but Ba hadn't understood a word for she beamed and nodded agreement. Even so, he felt his grandmother to be, in some way, under seige and that he should try to help. So with his heart beating fast, he advanced and said, 'Would you like another peardrop, if you please, ma'am?'

Aunt Evans moved slightly, ignoring the outstretched packet and putting her hand under his chin, moved it a little, so the light fell on his face.

'Goodness me!' she intoned, 'what beautiful eyes. Just like his mother's.'

As Llewelyn blushed and dropped his eyes, she seized his arm, pulled him close to her and, turning towards Ba, said in a loud whisper, 'Tell me, my little man, who is this old woman sitting next to me?'

He did his best to explain, but Aunt Evans' mind was like the surface of the Squire's pond, one minute calm and then, as though a stone had been hurled, broken and confused with the ripples reaching into all sorts of unexpected places. Determined, it seemed, to bring into the open as much of the past as possible, Aunt Evans passed Ba's life in review, and Llewelyn learned that his grandfather 'drank like a fish', that Ba and Aunt Evans were Liberals, that Ba used to tease her husband with a political slogan 'Orange for Ever, Blue in the Gutter', that he was 'a mad Tory' so that if an election was impending, he would give up his ship to fight the Tory cause, that he once fell drunk into the Gwaun River after a political meeting, was fished out, given a change of trousers from a local farmer, which he later kicked off with a roared protest that he wouldn't be seen dead in the breeks of a bloody Liberal and walked home in his Long Johns through the gawping town to the Ivy Bush, that he once paid a visiting German brass band a large fee to play 'Drink, Boys, Drink' as loudly as possible outside Bethel Chapel where one of Aunt Evans' Temperance gatherings was in progress (an act which it seemed Aunt Evans found difficult to forgive), and that Ba herself had once been taken home in a wheelbarrow from the Ivy Bush in something called a 'paralytic condition'.

Ba's unresponsive right ear filtered out most if not all of this, as it certainly did when Aunt Evans broke a momentary silence with, 'I heard Arthur made his money watering the beer in a Barry club', for Ba agreed with a smile.

'That's right, in Barry. Arthur and his wife Annie were very happy there.'

'A good deed and a just reward,' returned Aunt Evans severely.

When tea arrived, Nana must have sensed the tarnish which Aunt Evans had been spreading on the Acraman escutcheon, for when talk turned to Ba's father, she began, 'What a good man Granpapa was, Aunt Evans, and what a wonderful place The Plough store. I've heard it said that the farming in the whole district depended on 'The Plough'.

Aunt Evans regarded Nana closely with a light blue focusless stare, and then announced triumphantly, 'You must be Clara,' conferring on Nana the identity of her eldest (spinster) sister with whom she and Schoolin's wife were hardly ever on speaking terms for more than ten minutes on end.

'Dear me, no, Aunt Evans,' said the outraged Nana, 'I am Florrie, Florence Linda. Clara keeps a boarding house in Manchester.'

'God is not mocked you know,' said Aunt Evans solemnly.

Nor was the rest of the teatime conversation other than trying, with Nana and Llewelyn's mother seeking to head off the old lady from revelations.

While Schoolin was preparing the car for the return journey, Aunt Evans came back into focus, reached forward and placed her hand on Ba's, and said loudly enough this time, it seemed, for Ba to hear, 'You used to have a lovely alto voice, Joanna. I'd like to hear you sing 'Abide with Me' again.' And with the setting sun catching the jewelled rings on their joined withered hands, the two old ladies began to pipe the hymn in a reedy duet.

'Bravo, bravo,' said Schoolin who had just come in. 'Very well sung. But I'm afraid it's time to go.'

Nana, still rankling after Aunt Evans' confusion of her identity, remained unforgiving and unimpressed despite Schoolin's approval.

'Aunt Evans never could sing in tune,' she said after the visitor had gone, 'couldn't sing for toffee when she was young and still can't now she's old.'

'Not like Ba,' she added with a mixture of spite and satisfaction, pressing a piece of her denture-champing confection on her nephew.

Not all old ladies had families to care for them, a fact brought home to Llewelyn by a little drama which he never forgot, when

Schoolin took the family for a drive to Tenby, nearly forty miles away. As the family pulled up some twenty miles from the destination by a convenient gateway, through which Ba was slowly armed into the clover by Nana and his mother, Schoolin pointed to a silhouette only a few yards round the corner, but obscured from approaching cars by hedgetop gorsebushes. The figure was seated in an ancient Welsh armchair, wearing a man's peak cap pulled down over the face, shoulders beshawled Welsh fashion with a sack, and with a sack apron round the legs. The chair was sited on a little hedgerow platform, facing in the direction of Haverfordwest. It could have been either man or woman.

'Look,' said Schoolin. 'I knew we couldn't be far from her. It's the Old Lady. She's been sitting there for years, waiting for her son to come home from the Great War. He was killed the day before the Armistice.'

He spoke loudly, close to Ba's best ear.

'Poor dab', said the old lady, who had heard the story from Schoolin before, 'poor dab, to think of her sitting out there like that in all winds and weathers. What a lot I have to be thankful for. All the boys home safe and sound and Billy with all those medals. He always was the reckless one. I remember how he once rowed to the Fort in a tub . . .'

'Would you like to go up and see her?' Schoolin asked and when she nodded, the family made slow progression to the site. There was no embarrassment in staring at the Old Lady – she was the Old Lady to the end despite her scarecrow appearance – for with the peaked cap pressed down on her matted white locks, the eyes from which the light had long died out, staring without flicker, down the road to the station, she was unaware of gawping strangers. Her vigil had been so long that her chair looked part of the hedge, like the foxgloves and honeysuckle twining round the legs, and the buttercups which surrounded her feet. Ba regarded

her for a minute, her pursed lips moving slightly as though unable to find the right thing to say.

'Poor dab,' she said, and then lifting her voice a little, addressed the figure in quieter tones. 'I'm sorry your son has not come back, my dear. But I expect he will some day,' and with a sniff, she waddled painfully slowly on Schoolin's arm back to the Clyno.

On the beach, Ba and everybody guzzled their tongue sandwiches in sunshine and paddled in a sea warmed by hot sands. Then it began to rain and with hood up and side screens clipped on, the family started home. The Old Lady was still there, just visible through the smeared celluloid, sitting motionless in the rain, an additional sack over her head, still staring down the road to Haverfordwest, waiting for night when she would return to her tiny cottage, emerging at first light to resume her witness to the pity of war. She remained for years as a landmark in this part of Pembrokeshire, where today, no doubt, she would have been certified early on as in need of care and attention by well-meaning bureaucrats and taken forcibly out of the wind and rain of her vigil to die without hope.

Ba was armed to the Clyno for her last drive in her eighty-sixth year when Schoolin drove the family through the village of Puncheston to the Prescelly Mountains for the annual bilberry-picking expedition. He parked the car where Ba could sit and watch the pickers. It was a brilliant autumn day, the sky packed with shining, fleecy clouds. Llewelyn began to ply his grandmother with bilberries, carrying them in little empty sweet packets which she had kept specially for the purpose. While she ate, he got in by her side and taking the wheel drove down the narrow mountain road, gathering pace until he soared through the clouds over the Rosebush reservoir, past the derelict slate quarries, across the moors, past the fleeing sheep and mane-streaming ponies, over the dense woodland of the Gwaun Valley, and the red-funnelled Irish boats berthed in Fishguard Harbour, at speed over the heads of the bilberry harvesters.

To his astonishment, his grandmother said, 'We had a lovely drive, didn't we?'

There was no sign of anything wrong that evening as the family guzzled a pudding of bilberries, sealed in with boiled paste rich with chopped beef suet, which hung over the edge like the wig of a drunken advocate. But after Schoolin had armed Ba upstairs and Nana had helped her into bed, Nana reappeared and beckoned

Schoolin and his wife.

Minutes lengthened to half an hour before Schoolin returned with a frowning face. He looked at his son and said, 'Ba's got a bit of a bad old foot and she's very overtired. I'm going to Dr Ewen in the morning. It's a pity we haven't got the telephone in the village yet.'

Next morning, Nana said, holding and spreading her cards like a fan so Llewelyn could see for himself, 'I think it's going to be good news from Dr Ewen.'

Dr Ewen arrived an hour and a half later, a bustling short cheerful figure, but his expression as he left did not bear out Nana's morning prophecy. After his departure Schoolin drove a second time to Fishguard to buy bandages and ointments.

But Llewelyn never saw his grandmother again after the doctor's visit, and in the days that followed, Nana hung a curtain in the front of the bedroom door. The house was charged with the

reek of Winter Green, Schoolin began to rise earlier than his wont, to take his breakfast and walk to the garden and to roll and light and puff hard at his Shag cigarettes before he went into Ba's room. To the sweet strength of Winter Green was now added the concentrated smell of Jeyes Fluid and, from time to time, Nana burned brown-paper spills so that the smoke stayed on the landing. But a terrible presence hung in the air of the house. Later Llewelyn learned that Ba's foot had preceded her to the grave and was rotting away with gangrene and Schoolin had to dress the residues every morning. Soon there was no Ba anymore, only that dreaded presence . . .

One morning, Llewelyn heard Schoolin say to his mother, 'I hope poor old Ba doesn't go on much longer. I don't think I can stand much more. But her heart is so strong.'

The martyrdom that Ba's ending imposed on the house went on for so long that there was little grief left in anybody's heart by the time she died and was laid out for burial by Liza Moon, the village midwife who nursed the sick, comforted the dying, laid out the dead, solaced the bereaved; a huge bosomed figure in a Welsh woollen shawl and white scarf head-dress, whose caring spread round her like the sweet smell of apples.

But when the months of darkness came in, the empty chair left a yawning gap in the life and geography of the kitchen. Although she had been inactive for so long, the constancy and dependability of her white-haired, birdy-eyed presence had been a never-failing reassurance for all the family. From Ba, words always evoked loyal responses, cupped-ear nodding acquiescence or a smiling incomprehension which joined the family in a tolerant effort to explain. She was the least trying of any grandmother that ever was and remembrance that she had passed such happy secure days in the cosy corner bridewell of her old age, was a source of comfort to all when winter drove out the Indian summer in which she died.

CHAPTER FOURTEEN

Winter Shadows

'. . . the question of flooding of St Nicholas village was discussed . . .'
Minuties of the Parish Council Meeting, 25 April 1930

'. . . it was decided to ascertain from the Electric Light Company,
the conditions on which an electricity supply could be brought
to St Nicholas.'
Minutes of the Parish Council Meeting, 28 November 1930

Winter was above all the season of early darkness. It came in like
a tide and drowned the village. The rain became wet darkness,
the gale black wind. Passersby in the village street called goodnight
to identify themselves and receive evidence of identity in return,
a habit of greeting which those brought up in country districts or
unillumined villages never entirely lose. They walked by memory,
avoiding the bumps and ruts, the potholes and broken ground.
The only break in the blackness was the smoky summons of the
shop window, the weak glare of cottage candles, the beam of an
occasional torch, the knee-high bobbing glow of a hurricane
lantern, the yellow light of the carbide bicycle lamp.

The moon eased the countryman's lot a little; rendered it easier
to walk down the garden to the silvery closet, sited well away from
the house for sound olfactory reasons, to make the Sunday journey
to winter evensong, to fetch the forgotten can of water from the
well, recognise and loiter and briefly gossip, to eke out the life of
day. To refer to a 'beautiful night' meant as much as anything

that one could see a neighbour's face, read and recognise the approaching silhouette. The phase of the moon was a factor always considered in deciding the dates and times of meetings. There was no warranty the moon would appear, but the hope was there.

But although the moon in its waxing phases blunted the edges of darkness, the blackness in between turned the village in on itself and many personal relationships became rancid. Whereas on light evenings, women stood on doorsteps or met in groups in the street to talk and gossip, they now began to visit each other's homes in ones and twos, with an almost desperate frequency, and in the insidious gloom the gossip and rumour-mongering grew and wavered like some corrupt Jack o' Lantern.

As a consequence, winter was invariably the season of quarrels. They arose from a multiplicity of causes, the rumoured loose behaviour of a daughter or son, a husband's roving eye, accusations of a dirty house, neglect of a parent, laziness, talking in grandiose terms about a (territorially) distant relative, birth out of wedlock, debt, and the throat-biting tittle tattle, either without foundation or grossly distorted, invariably got back to the victim, though one

could not always ascertain how. But while these were immediate
triggers it was the boredom and claustrophobia imposed by
darkness which was mainly responsible for the explosions.

Battle was joined out of doors, either from doorstep positions,
or at a distance of twenty to thirty yards in the village street, the
insults hurled like bullets in a Western gunfight, venomously
personal missiles, with just enough truth to wound and worry. The
fights were all-women affairs, the men either at work or, at most,
hovering vaguely nearby, and sheepishly muted too when they
passed each other in the street, or met, briefly and wordlessly,
in the shop.

For the first few days after a battle, the village remained more or
less aloof. Then the trauma began to throb, heads to shake, the
collective heart to drop a few beats. The violence brought an initial
burst of excitement, leavened veins sluggish with winter boredom,
with a quick shot of adrenalin. But the village, despite the
disagreements inseparable from community life, could not tolerate
for long such a hole in the life fabric. So the peacemaking began.

Schoolin's wife often played a role and she felt especially
strongly about one quarrel which was triggered by a particularly
nasty and totally untrue rumour.

'I think I'll take Daisy a pot of jelly,' she said to Schoolin, and
walked with self-consciously erect carriage up the village street,
dressed in her second-best clothes which seemed to her to strike
the right note. Although the role of peacemaker nourished her
sense of family superiority, as someone who stood above the
common altercations of the village, she was genuinely grieved for
those who were embroiled, especially on this ugly occasion.

'Hello, Daisy,' she said, 'we were just going to start the bramble
jelly. It should be good this year because the blackberries had
plenty of sun. I said to Mr Jones, I thought you would like to
try it.'

She placed the gift on the table. 'And how are you, Daisy?'

G

Before Daisy, thin and wiry, white-faced with large brown eyes, straggly straight grey hair, pinafored and clogged could reply, Catherine continued, 'I've been thinking a lot about you lately.'

Her gaze, always disconcertingly direct, took on an intensive quality as though she were willing the thought reference to the quarrel into Daisy's mind. Meeting Catherine's shining, brown eyes could be a disturbing experience.

Daisy's own grey eyes faltered a moment. 'I know you are talking about Mary Cowan, Mrs Jones,' she said. 'I shan't never speak to her again as long as I live. You don't know what she 'ave told about me.'

In fact Catherine and the whole village and much of the parish knew, although the actual public quarrel had taken on the form of personal abuse, and the reputed major insult, the sinister *causus belli*, had not been mentioned in the street set-to, but sent whispering through the village.

As though unable to contain it any longer, Daisy blurted, with tight-lips and flashing eyes, 'She said I 'ad something nasty the matter with me and that was why Danny 'ad gone away.'

Weary of the low agricultural wage, Danny had indeed packed up his job and gone for two weeks to stay with a brother who was a coal-trimmer in Cardiff docks, to investigate employment

possibilities, leaving his wife with a quarter pig and a garden of vegetables to keep the family body together in his absence.

Catherine had already got to the bottom of this uniquely unpleasant rumour, and knew how the misunderstanding had arisen.

A few months before, an elderly farm worker, long noted for his queer ways, had taken to his bed, displayed symptoms of madness which had been diagnosed on his death-bed as arising from an early untreated venereal disease contracted abroad when he was a sailor. His childless wife, sad, secretive, never seen out-of-doors, always dressed in her Welsh shawl and a closely pinned high woollen scarf, had reputedly shown the doctor the ravages of her throat which made her shun the light. It had been a violent end and Isaiah had been called in by the doctor to help control the patient, who was a steady churchgoer, as he fought the phantasmagoria round his deathbed.

The widow's Christian and surnames were identical with Daisy's and the recipient of Mary Cowan's gossip, deaf and not too bright, had confused the two identities of Daisy and the same-name widow. The old gossip's misinterpretation, repeated to Daisy, had festered and built up pus in the winter darkness, until explosion point was reached and the poison scattered abroad in a noisy quarrel. With patient therapy Catherine was able, not for the first nor last time, to heal the wounds.

Winter meant rain, and for a whole day and night the November downfall had pelted and sheeted into the parish. The village was literally awash, the gullies roaring and pouring down the main street, every house under watery siege.

The first to stir were those who had business on the farms. David Evans, thin and wiry as an ivy trunk, sat on the side of the bed, levered his legs in their long underpants (which he never took off except to put on the other pair once a month) into cold corduroy trousers. As he laced up his oiled leather boots, he listened resignedly to the downpour volleying against his two-roomed cottage window. His wife was just stirring, his twelve-year-old daughter fast asleep in the tiny curtained-off corner, the two boys up the ladder under the eaves. No room anywhere, not enough to swing a bloody rabbit. He placed the candle on the table, and putting a sack over his head stumbled in the darkness down the garden path to the closet.

His wife was up when he returned, lifting the big iron kettle off the culm fire where it had been heating since four o'clock. She got out of bed every night to put it on. She was a damn good woman and deserved better. Twenty-eight and six he got last week for six days' work. His boss was mean as a winkie. He'd leave him tomorrow, the old skinflint, except there was no other work, except perhaps the quarry. He wouldn't want that. He drank his tea with condensed milk, ate the two buns, put his packet of bread, a bit of cheese and an onion and two more buns into his pocket, scraped a chew off his lump of twist, manoeuvering it comfortably in his cheek, donned the oilskin and the hat which his wife had skimped to buy, checked the carbide and water in his lamp and set off through the deluge to his half past six beginning of the day's work.

Down the street, the smallholders and their wives too were getting up, the roadman and his wife were downstairs, and Meiriog and Martha were dressing.

The three rabbit trappers had been out of their houses since before six, sackclothed and oilskinned, riding slowly through the merciless rain with only the yellow wavering beam of their carbide lamps to guide them through the pelting darkness. They carried lengths of binder twine in their pockets, small home-made truncheons, and their bicycles were fitted with wooden frames over the handlebars and the back wheels.

Dafydd Moon, pushing open the first gate on Tresissillt Farm just after six, leant his bicycle against the hedge. He took the carbide lamp off his bicycle and began his rounds, illuminating his traps with the yellow beam. The rain beat on his clothes. What a morning. Many of the morning's rabbits were dead, or drained of movement by the pain of broken legs, coupled with numbing cold rain. Holding each rabbit by the ears as he bent over the trap,

Dafydd opened the gins with his boot, killed as required with a quick cutting side blow of his hard experienced palm and bundled the rabbits into the sack. He used his truncheon twice only – for a weasel, its tiny leg held by a shred of sinew only but still defiant and dangerous, and for a buzzard, huge though bedraggled, hissing defiance and flapping its great speckled wings.

He wheeled the two heavy sacks of rabbits to the farm barn through pools of yard water, took off his oilskins, and reached into his pocket for the bacon sandwiches which Liza provided each morning for his breakfast in the farm kitchen. Dammo. Dammo and dammo again. Now he remembered he had left his sandwich tin in the outhouse, when fetching his bike. Dammo. That meant going home for breakfast and coming back all the way again to re-set the traps. He hoped Liza wouldn't worry if she had found them. Oh well. He shrugged his shoulders, and rolled and lit a cigarette. Then he lit the hurricane lamp, opened the razor-sharp blade of his knife, and slit the soaked paunch of the first bedraggled rabbit with the razor-sharp steel. He hung each leg-joined couple on the collecting line as he set about completing the evisceration of the night's harvest.

Through the water-gorged clouds, grey as the weather-beaten granite of Garn Fawr, the light of the morning had at last begun to percolate. But the rain was still falling in sheets, there was no sense of a new day beginning and the cowled, sackclothed and oilskinned figures moving around the farms and roads looked like wraiths from the life and work of yesterday.

Back in the village, the sound of water roaring down the street was even louder and though every window was now shining with candlelight, every door was still fast closed. Liza Moon, the village midwife, with automatic lifeless gestures, made a pot of tea and

cut a slice of bread and butter. She did not eat or drink but sat with her head in her hands. Once again, for the third time in a fortnight, Bryn's bed had not been slept in. She had until this morning discounted the stories, believed him that he had been with friends in Fishguard but now in her thudding heart she knew the gossip was true. A wave of self-pity, bitter as gall, flooded through her and her eyes began to water.

That bitch, that ugly, grinning bitch, that filthy *whooren*, with her painted face and silk stockings and her tits held up like an old cow's udder. Ugh a fi, ugh a fi. What did Bryn, clean and handsome as a prince, want with shit like that when any nice girl would be prepared to have him. Oh God help her. Why did he have to do this to a mother who had tried so hard to do everything in her power for him ever since his father died. She even married Dafydd to give Bryn a proper home. Tears fell and rolled down the deep smile creases of her pale fleshy cheeks and she wiped them away with her apron. Another wave of grief and self-pity swept through her.

She began to wail loudly and, suddenly fearful she might be heard, placed her hand over her mouth and laid her head on the scrubbed wood of the table letting her body shake and rack with muffled sobs. Then came a thought that drove out the grief, and

brought a terrible pain under her thumping left breast. What about the *sin*. Last Sunday the minister at Harmony had preached a sermon of smoking denunciation of the rising number of affiliation orders at Mathry Petty Sessions during the year, had thundered the doom of all whores and fornicators in the parish. He consigned each and all of them to eternal fire, unless they repented, sought the forgiveness of the Saviour who had taken the sins of men on himself and sacrificed himself for their sake. *Sacrifice.*

Liza's breath came in gasps, the pain in her side now so fierce, the beat of her heart so clamorous that she had to cup her huge drooping bosom with the big, strong, mottled hands which had smoothed so many pillows, touched the bowed heads of so much grief, composed so many twisted masks of death into the semblance of peace to comfort the living. *Suddenly she knew what she must do.* It was like a light from Heaven, a terrible light, and a flood of tears which she would never have guessed were still there after her early weeping, deluged down her face, and as one who has cared and comforted all her life and well knew the value of tears, she let herself weep and weep.

Then with her grief and fear washed away, she lifted her shawl over her head to keep off the rain, and went out to the little shed to fetch what she needed from Dafydd's bench to do what she had to do – for Bryn.

Pedalling slowly through the rain, Dafydd cycled over the rough footpath bridge across Tresissillt River and up the rise to the village. The deluge and the discomfort were immediately transcended and forgotten as he thought of his paragon. Liza would be surprised to see him. How did an ordinary chap like Dafydd Moon, just a simple rabbit trapper with no looks or brains and only just over five foot tall, come to win a beauty like Liza! What a glory and a joy it had been when she agreed to marry him.

It always had been and always would be a wonder and a mystery.

Dafydd forgot the rain and the hill and his hunger, and his bike flew until he turned into his tiny yard. As he thought, there were his sandwiches by the window. He took off his oilskins, removed the wet sack from round his legs, wiped his boots clean carefully so as not to dirty Liza's clean floor. The kitchen was dark but as he entered he saw Liza hanging from the hook in the kitchen beam with her feet almost touching the floor. She was making a terrible slobbering, choking sound and Dafydd lifted her in his arms back on to the chair and with a superhuman effort held her while he undid the terrible knot and laid her gently on the floor. She was alive thank God, thank God, for she was mumbling in Welsh, 'Leave me die, for Bryn's sake, great God, leave me die . . .' and weeping and gasping.

In terror that she would die, he put a cushion under her head and rushed to Schoolin's house, opened the door and cried, 'Come quick, come quick, Liza's hanged herself . . .' Schoolin rose from the table and rushed out with Dafydd, and Llewelyn ran upstairs

to tell his mother who came down in her nightdress. She put on Schoolin's coat and a pair of slippers and, throwing a towel over her head, followed Schoolin, with her young son behind. To Llewelyn, palpitating and breathless, Liza, lying on the floor with terrible red weals round her neck and her clothes all awry, looked like a huge rag doll. His mother pulled down Liza's clothes, and said to Dafydd, 'Get some water and bathe her poor throat. Poor soul, poor soul, whatever made her do it?'

Dafydd, his breath coming in gasps, his face like the colour of flour said, 'She did it because of Bryn. I heard her say so.'

Schoolin's wife, who knew all about the gossip of Bryn's involvement with the Wicked Woman of the parish who lived half a mile out of the village, underlined her knowledge with her reply. 'I know. Liza is a very proud woman, Mr Moon, a very proud woman.' Catherine's face shone as she said, 'I know what it means to be proud . . .'

Schoolin, who had been taking Liza's pulse, examining her throat, feeling her brow, said, 'Now,' his hand on Dafydd's shoulder, 'Dafydd, you don't have to worry any more, Liza's going to be all right. D'you understand? All right. But I think you ought to get Dr Ewen to examine her. I'll go and get him if you like. He'll be as quiet as the grave.'

Lips trembling and his eyes overflowing with tears, Dafydd began to bathe his wife's throat with stricken gentleness. 'I'll never be able to thank God enough for this,' he gasped. 'And thank you, Mr Jones bach.'

Schoolin said in a low urgent voice to his wife, 'I don't think we ought to be here when Liza is herself again. Then she will think nobody knows except Dafydd.'

In fact the whole village already knew, for a passerby had seen Schoolin and his wife running to the back door, and a number were already standing in the pouring rain with shocked faces as Schoolin and his wife and Llewelyn came out. Urgently and quickly, Schoolin explained the need for secrecy and silence and ushered them away, after extracting solemn promises of discretion.

As so often, the compassionate Schoolin's reading of the human heart was right, for when Liza came round, she asked Dafydd whether anybody had seen her or knew about her attempt at self-destruction. Nobody at all except for him, Dayfdd lied with all the love at his command, and Liza made him fetch the Bible and place his hand on it and swear a great oath that he was telling the truth. The need for secrecy was carried round the village by the

parish deacons, supported by the ministers and the rector, and the doctor fetched by Schoolin agreed to keep silent. The village closed its ranks and buried the memory.

Liza lived, but the rope had destroyed something rare and precious for ever. She gave up her role of village comforter, went no more to chapel, began to read threatening auguries and dire omens in innocent events, and to fear death greatly. When a blackbird flew against her bedroom window, she insisted that Dafydd blow it to bits with his gun. Then with one of those tragic twists which give life its bitter irony, her son, who had turned over a new leaf after the attempted suicide, fell from the roof on a building site and was brought home to die. For two years thereafter, she sat by the fire, tended hand and foot and heart by her doting Dafydd. To her visitors she would say in a dead voice, looking through the little trapper as though he were not present at all, 'You see, I've nothing left. I've lost everything. Everything I valued in life.'

Her last words to Dafydd were to bury her with Bryn who was already lying with his father in the cemetery under Garn Fawr.

Middle-aged Liza died of a broken heart. Young sick people of the parish of those days were more likely to die of consumption, produce of the endless winter rain, and not enough to eat. Jimmy the little Mole King coughed himself into a bloody sputum grave at sixteen, his two sisters joined him at eighteen and twenty years of age. That was a bitterly sad home, for apart from the grim ravages of consumption and the death of Cyril in the hayfield, the last son was drowned at sea.

In the village, the tailor lost three of his four children through consumption, one in her late teens, two in their early twenties. He was the poorest man in the village, with a household that literally starved. He charged three shillings for making a flannel shirt and a pound for making a suit and he worked furiously and unrelentingly when work was available and delivered it on foot up to ten miles away. But work was scarce and for hours on end he sat in the window in the cross-legged posture of his trade, pale, hollow-cheeked, thin as a bamboo, and stared into space.

The other adult scourge was melancholia, known by the derisive name of 'vallen'. The 'vallen' always had a culpable ring and men and women took to their beds and stayed there, in some cases for twenty years, until death brought release to victim and family.

CHAPTER FIFTEEN

Larks in the Snow

*'It was unanimously agreed that the Christmas holidays should
commence on 22nd December and that the children were expected
to return on 2nd January 1929.'*

School Managers' Minutes, 24 July 1928

That same year, four days before Christmas, the feathers of billions
of celestial geese fluttered down from an invisible pewter-coloured
sky and buried the parish of St Nicholas under a deep thick mantle.
Everything in the village suddenly became shabby. The Roman
geese about to lose their own feathers and until then the whitest in
the parish, seemed to have been sprinkled with wood ash. The
dazzling white fur on John John's cat Gabriel took on a murky
shade. The lime wash on Clogs' cottage walls, that always seemed
to equal in purity the white foam on the breaking Abermawr
combers, turned grey. Even Schoolin's white collars, soaked in
Robin starch, glazed to osseous stiffness with cauterising strokes
of Nana's fire irons (on which readiness-checking spit disintegrated
into dancing hobgoblins), took on an ashen hue.

But the snow, whose virginal shine mocked the physical
cleanliness of the village, had a distinctly cleansing and calming
effect on the minds and hearts of the inhabitants, as though it had
poulticed and drawn the inflammation from the throbbing wens
of winter grievance. Life became communal again from experiences
shared: digging out the old school cleaner's front door, freeing the

cottage entrance of a dying consumptive, concerned speculation about the plight of isolated moorland dwellers.

The morning after the blizzard, Llewelyn woke at his usual time, and for a moment thought it was night. He had moved into the bedroom with the skylight, which today was buried beneath a foot of snow. He heard sounds in the kitchen and got out of bed, dressed by the light of his torch and descended the stairs. In the kitchen the fire was blazing, lamp lit, the kettle softly singing over the dozing cats. Nana looked up from her first card reading divinations of the day.

She pointed with the Ace of Spades and spoke in a dramatic tone. 'Hallo, Llewelyn. Have you seen the snow? Look, it's almost up to the window. Your father is clearing a way to the fowls. They haven't even been fed yet.'

Her gaze travelled from the partly blocked window, resting for a moment on the hanging flitches, shoulders and hams that filled the kitchen with the pendulous promise of feasts to come.

'Ah,' she said with a thankful inflection, 'isn't it a good thing poor Blodwen's gone. The snow by the pigsty is as high as a mountain. She'd have had to wait such a long time for her breakfast, poor thing.'

An excited Llewelyn hardly took in his aunt's remarks as he gobbled his breakfast, and then on Nana's orders, mittened, double-stockinged, over-coated and scarved, he opened the back door.

He met a dazzling winter world already lit by the weak morning sun. Dragon-breathed, he jumped up the steps, walked along the chasm excavated by Schoolin, who was now driving a way to the closet with urgent sweeps of his long-handled Welsh shovel.

Llewelyn was thrilled with joy and excitement at the gigantic masses, the dazzling unlimited tons of soft, malleable material which were his to do with as he liked. He picked up a double handful, threw it in the air, just as the first familiar summons of the day sounded from next door. Tusks was giving normal notice of his arrival on the scene, with a stick dragged along the corrugations on the zinc shed.

He materialised behind the wire-netting fence. He was, by any standards, oddly garbed. Over his overcoat he was draped in a hessian smock fashioned from a hundredweight sack, with a hole for his head, and reaching almost to his heels where it sported a large hem. Round the middle he was girdled with binder twine, like a friar's tassel. His eldest sister, who had recently read about dress designing in the *Sunday Companion* had used the first material to hand, for her initial attempt at *haute couture*.

He climbed on to a box to peer over into Schoolin's yard. 'Coo,' he said, 'in'it deep. Deeper'n the sea.'

He jumped off and sank into the snow so that his legs disappeared completely under his smock. He looked through the netting, and as though he had just completed an important computation, said, rather solemnly, 'We got more'n you.' He waved vaguely towards the sentry box closet in his backyard. 'We got three and a 'alf tons,' he said finally, like some loony midget millionaire. In extricating himself from where he had sunk in the snow, he fell on his face.

Llewelyn said, 'I'll see you out front. I've got a threepennybit from my aunt.'

Galvanised by peardrops and bullseye visions, Tusks rose and staggered like an inebriated gnome through the backyard hillocks.

The wind in the night had blown the snow into drifts against the houses, but the road was passable and the two friends trudged through towards the shop where the drifts covered even the peardrops and bullseyes in the window, though a groaning Bilbow had already cleared a passage to the door. A minute later, mouths stopped with hot stripey sugary balls, Tusks and Llewelyn emerged from the redolent gloaming to the blinding world outside, to find Collars, Clogs and Gwilym Thomas of the deadly hand and eye approaching the store.

Collars stopped a few feet away and examined the sack clothed Tusks with genuine astonishment. Then a slow grin burgeoned above his celluloid collar and, putting his hands out in mock alarm, he shied violently and shouted, 'Look out, it's the bloomin' bwcki-bo' – the mysterious dreaded creature which was supposed to haunt the countryside of those days (often used by hard-pressed mothers to threaten disobedient children). Then the gang, including Llewelyn, now swept into treacherous abandonment of his friend, shouted out, 'The bwcki-bo, the bloomin' bwcki-bo' and began to stagger round an isolated Tusks, the sentinels of whose smile appeared alarmingly yellow in the snow.

The fun over, Gwilym Thomas bent down, scooped up a double handful of snow and pressed and rounded the mass until it was hard as a cricket ball. A faintly uncertain expression appeared on the faces of his companions, but Gwilym had other targets in mind that morning. Following the forced sale of the family farm, he carried a heavy chip of grievance against society on his burly young shoulders.

He looked round. 'Eighteen sixty blooming six' he said, reading the date on the chapel and the white thunderbolt exploded and

splattered the plaque. He made another ball and it disintegrated against a rook's nest, filling the Squire's plantation with a loud chorus of wings and caws. His next missile burst above the west window of the church.

'Time for the bloomin' school now,' he said, and led the way in a plunging run to the school playground. Here he moulded six new balls, blowing on his cupped fists in between to drive out the cold.

The boys stood in front of Miss Prothero's classroom staring up at the silent bell.

'One, two blooming three,' counted Gwilym and the little bell tinkled in response, as it did three times more, before Collars shouted, in mock alarm, 'Look out by there, it's the Schoolin,' and led the way, in a staggering escaping run. Gwilym's powerful bare legs bore him through the deep snow, with Collars close on his sinking heels, but Clogs failed, albeit valiantly, to keep up, and Llewelyn gave up completely when Tusks finally fell on his face, arms buried up to his elbows.

Meanwhile Gwilym and Collars had reached the smithy where the mandrils and the discarded rusting piles of old iron had been completely buried by the blizzard, although the thick carpet on the roof was already beginning to show first faint signs of movement as the heat of the forge rose through the grimy ceiling.

The boys stood in the doorway. Shirt-sleeved, waist-coated Meiriog paused for a second in his bellows-blowing, gave them a quick glance and said, 'Hello, you boys. You can come in out of the cold, if you like.'

He pointed to a vacant place.

A match flared in the gloaming, and the Reverend Isaiah's face was highlighted for a moment as he puffed his home-rolled 'Royal Seal' fag into a glowing end. Another match flowered, revealing the farmer Harold Binyon, whose saddled weight-carrying cob was tied to the ring in the forge wall, and whose broken tug-chain Meiriog was raising to white heat in the fire, before welding. The farmer sucked the flame noisily into the charred reeking bowl of his pipe, igniting the pungent flaked twist, blowing out smoke as strong almost as those clouds of nitrogenous burnt hoof that filled the forge on shoeing days.

He continued with an already begun saga of the snow.

'I don't reckon I've ever seen so many rabbits in a field as I saw on the way in, in Parc-y-Coed,' he said. 'I didn't count them. But there must have been two hundred, I reckon. Sitting in the snow.'

There was a loud gasp from the shadows. Isaiah, who had called in to discuss clearing a path to the church with his church warden and stayed on for a gossip, gripped the ends of his sleeves in both hands and held his arms out wide from his body.

'You don't say,' he said. 'You don't say. Actually sitting in the snow. *Two hundred*?'

Then as the scene registered itself fully in his mind, he forgot himself completely. '*Two hundred*,' he repeated, 'Good God.'

The problems of the Sabbath completely in eclipse, scattering exclamations like a bursting snowball, he left the smithy, turned right and proceeded as fast as he could through the snow to tell Schoolin the news. Ten minutes later, in shooting macs and headgear, twelve-bore shotguns under their arms, they rendezvous-ed by the smithy and went past the shop, down the white road towards Parc-y-Coed, half a mile away.

Without a word, hardly noticed by the smith and the farmer, now chuckling together at the spectacle of the departing pair, Gwilym left the smithy followed by Collars. Llewelyn, Clogs and Tusks had arrived outside but Gwilym swept them contemptuously aside, with a gesture of his left arm and said, 'We don't want you lot hanging around. Push off.'

Then he cupped his hand in the familiar conspiratorial manner which usually presaged his particular brand of mayhem, and said, 'Follow me, Collars. We're going to 'ave some fun, boy. Some fun.'

They turned into the narrow lane behind the shop and while Schoolin and Isaiah walked the two sides, they struggled through the snow along the short-cut hypotenuse, to be first in the field. Parc-y-Coed was a hunter's dream, being fronted by one of the very few tree copses in the parish, an ideal place for an approaching marksman to instal himself unseen. The boys were in position well before the two macintoshed figures moved among the lower trees, long enough in fact for Gwilym to prepare five of his hard missiles of moulded snow. He hefted the first firmly and lovingly in his big left palm, as unmindful of the cold as the rabbits were of the approaching menace in the trees, their normally hair-triggered danger-alerting senses numbed by cold and hunger. Schoolin had now taken up position near the lower end of the copse and a crouching Isaiah had approached within twenty yards of the boys, themselves securely hidden behind a bush of briars.

Then, having raised his hand with care and caution, in an agreed signal to the watching, waiting Schoolin, Isaiah picked his own targets for a left and right and lifted his gun slowly to take aim – just as the first hard snowball, propelled with the force and accuracy of a catapult, took him painfully on his left ear. At the

same moment, Schoolin's left and right barrels roared death at his successfully selected victims, and the whole field suddenly came to life as a brown flood of escaping rabbits scored the snow with a fantasia of hieroglyphics.

The rabbits were, however, still just within gunshot, but before an astonished Isaiah – having cast a quick glance in the direction of the attack – could take quick aim, a second missile thudded home and removed his hat. Genuinely alarmed now, Isaiah was lowering his gun when, with a raucous cry, two superb cock pheasants, their plumage made even more brilliant by the background of sunlit snow, suddenly exploded from the nearby undergrowth. They planed flush across his line of vision, and with the swift deadly reflexes of the born and experienced marksman, his gun flashed to his shoulder, and with a left and right, he brought the two birds tumbling into the snow.

Forgetful now of everything except his poacher's loot, Isaiah rushed from his vantage, and Collars and Gwilym, now concerned only with their own escape, ran from their hiding place towards the gate. Then Schoolin arrived, holding the material of two rabbit pies in his right hand. But his grin of triumph changed rapidly to one of astonishment (not entirely free of chagrin either)

when he took in the gleaming plumage of the dead pheasants in Isaiah's right hand.

'Good God, Isaiah,' he said, 'where did you get those?'

Grinning, overflowing with joy, scattering and splashing explanations like wedding confetti in the snow, Isaiah was about to reply when he suddenly remembered the recent train of events.

'Schoolin bach,' he said, 'a most extraordinary thing. I was about to shoot my two rabbits, when I was struck two powerful blows from afar.'

He pointed to his porkpie hat still lying in the snow and then touched his ear, wincing painfully. He withdrew his hand, pointing to a speck of blood.

'Look,' he said in a reproachful tone, 'it's blood.'

Suddenly, he pointed with his empty gun. 'There,' he said sharply, 'look, look there they go,' as Collars and Gwilym, unrecognisable in overcoats and caps from that back-view distance, disappeared through the gateway.

Schoolin's famous stentorian roared across the snow in menacing pursuit.

'Hey there, you boys, come back here at once.' But they were gone. Schoolin, versed in assigning names to examples of characteristic mischief, could have sworn he recognised the Gwilym Thomas style.

Then as though the spirit of goodwill from the approaching Christmas season had healed his injuries, removed the offence, ousted the remaining vestiges of his wrath, and filled him with forgiveness, Isaiah began to chuckle, gripping his sleeves and holding out his arms.

'Ha . . . hm . . . hm . . . ha! A pair of rascals. Snowballs hey!

Can't think who they were. Snowballing the rector. Hm . . .
hm . . . he. We've all been wicked in our time, I suppose. Ha . . .
hm.'

Gleefully, he lifted and hefted the shining plumaged birds,
placed his gun against a tree, and his face grew solemn. 'God
moves in a mysterious way,' he said. 'If I hadn't been struck, I'd
never have got these two beauties.' He looked at Schoolin's rabbits.
'I'd only have had a pair of rabbits like you, Schoolin,' he added.

Now he began to stow the loot of his left and right barrels in
his left and right poacher's pocket.

'I thought, if you don't mind, I'd carry one of your rabbits,
Schoolin,' he said. 'Then if we meet the bobby, it will all look
quite natural. Ha . . . hm . . . ho . . . ho. Yes. Hm . . . ha.'

They turned for home. Half way to the village, Isaiah stopped,
gave a great grin which exposed his tobacco-stained teeth, gently
slapped his pheasant-cushioned right thigh and said, 'What a
Christmas! A brace of pheasants for Christmas Day. Now I can
sell the geese in the Fishguard Christmas Market for good hard
cash. Ho . . . ha . . . hm. Boy oh boy. What a Christmas!'

Cash was also the subject which, the next day, brought Collars,
his brother Croakers, Clogs, Voices, Llewelyn and Tusks into
carolling conclave in front of the village shop. The sun was
beginning to sink in the sea and a huge new sovereign moon was
poised in the sky ready to float over the white countryside.

It was colder, for the temperature had hardly risen above
freezing all day; there was a brilliant sparkle on the snow, which
produced a general jumping up and down and windmilling of arms.

Collars spoke. 'We'll start with the bloomin' Squire. Croakers
'as got 'is mouth organ. Ee don't sing.'

213

His eyes ranged over the rest of the choir in the gathering gloom. 'Voices,' he said, 'your father is a conductor. So you'll start us hoff. One, two, three, see? Count with your harms. Like this –' and Collars flailed his right arm up and down.

'We'll start with 'Wild Shepherds' and if 'e wants more we'll give 'm Wesley's Slash.'

His gaze settled on Tusks and he wrinkled his nose in vague disapproval. 'You, Tusks,' he said, 'you'll just do bloomin' la's.'

Collars had made a good choice of carols, for the Big School had learned these two for the end of Christmas term sing-song and the older ones could still even produce the rudimentary harmonising which Schoolin had taught them.

Led by Collars, loudly whistling the first carol, they trouped in ragged procession down the road and reached the Squire's kitchen just as the cook was about to close the door, after letting in the cat.

'Hallo,' she said, 'are you the singers then? You better sing inside, isn't it? It's too cold for you out there.'

So they stood in a solemn semi-circle before the pulsing culm fire in the kitchen inglenook, with Voices standing a pace in front, vaguely in charge.

As his arm fell for the third time the little choir began to sing. It was a rather ragged beginning but quickly became a surprisingly mellifluous sound, with an overtone of alto harmony contributed by Voices and one or two daring snatches of remembered descant from Llewelyn's high soprano. Collars was about to put an end to this uppityness by Schoolin's son with a hard, hidden pinch on his bottom when the door into the main part of the house opened, and the white-bearded Squire stood in the doorway. He looked stern and forbidding, but his bleak chairman-of-the-bench expression seemed to soften as the children's voices unfolded the song of the Nativity in his kitchen. They sang it through to the end and then, supporting himself with his gold-headed stick, he limped into the kitchen, a frightening figure of authority even in his own home. But his voice, though stern and clipped, was not unkind.

'Very good, boys,' he said. 'Very good indeed.' His piercing brown eyes under their high, arching white eyebrows identified the children one by one as the sons of their respective fathers.

'Do you know any more?' he asked and he watched and listened

with an expression almost of pleasure as they gave him the saga of King Wenceslas through all its verses, to the final homily.

He put his hand in his pocket and a shower of five silver sixpences fell on the scrubbed table. 'Merry Christmas, boys,' he said and limped away.

'Merry Christmas, sir,' came the chorus.

At the door, he turned. 'See they have plenty to eat, Lilian,' he said. 'It's a cold night.'

So they sat at the long table and stuffed themselves with mince pies and Welsh cakes and bowls of Welsh flummery and cream, washed down with the teetotal Squire's ginger beer. Tusks spoke for all of them when he produced a vast involuntary belch which came roaring through his absent teeth as though he were a camel.

They emerged into the sparkling night and did the rest of the village with the animation of crusaders, stowing the money inside Collars' pocket where it jangled reassuringly when they ran. They came last of all to the tailor. There was no money here, but the

tall cadaverous Englishman had taken six of his empty cotton reels,
pared the bodies down to points at one end and inserted a circular
pointed stem, like a pencil, which protruded at the pared end.
Coloured red, white and blue, they were surely some of the most
beautiful finger tops in the world, and after the tailor had
demonstrated with pale-faced glee how, after touring the table in
a wide curving sweep, the top would move towards the table centre
and then go silently 'to sleep' – or by a flick of the fingers could
be made to gyrate like an inverted toadstool on its stalk – he
wished them a merry Christmas and let them out through the
front door.

The gang stood for a moment in the village street, breathing like
dragons in the icy moonlight, buoyed and cocky and exuberant
with the evening's successes.

The leader surveyed his troops, and came to a sudden decision.
There was still time to seek new worlds to conquer.

'I'll tell yer wot, you lot,' he said, 'I'll tell yer wot. Let's go to
sing in Llangloffan.

'*Llangloffan*. Gosh. Three miles away.'

A shudder of excitement went through the choir.

But before any response or argument could be offered, Collars
was away down the road with the rest of them in his wake.

They never got to Llangloffan that evening, however, for when
they reached the big chapel cemetery and stood for a moment
staring at the snow-covered tombstones shining in the moon, a
loud contralto voice with the hint of a sob came from among the

sepulchres, singing the most famous of the hymns composed by
William Lewis, the hymnologist of nearby Abermawr.

In that white silent world the effect was totally eerie and
terrifying and the boys stood petrified into stone.

Then Clogs with a great gasp and with his hand to his mouth
said, 'It's the singing of the dead,' and before he had finished his
terrible judgement, Collars Morgan was away down the road,
racing back the way they had come.

Hardly could it be said that he was leading his troops for his
longer stronger legs rapidly outpaced those of his fellow carollers,
especially that little camp follower of the night, the terrified and
tearful Tusks, to whose deserted side a palpitating Llewelyn now
returned, to seize him by the hand and drag him lurching and
stumbling, well beyond his fastest achievable speed, towards the
safety of the village and home.

The snow provided a magic back cloth to the glories and goodies
which arrived in Bilbow's store three weeks before the Great Day.
In the light of the hanging lamp which danced on the snow outside
the window, the shop was transfigured into an Aladdin's Cave for
the children. The ceiling suddenly sprouted stalactites, dripping
with treasure, gauze stocking cornucopias filled with paper hats
and streamers and raucous sirens that blew out like striking
cobras, and balloons and clay bubble pipes and shining metal
puzzles and miniature snakes and ladders, draughts and happy
families and rainbow transfers, and picture stories and celluloid
ducks and tin whistles and mouth organs and baby xylophones and
tiny pots and pans and miniature rolling pins and weighing scales
and mirrors and monkeys and hurdy-gurdies and jig-saws and
chocolate coins.

The sweet jars were topped and ready, liquorice pipes, sweet
cigarettes and sherbet prominent on the counter and, for the big
spenders, boxes of red-ribbon-tied 'King George V' chocolates.
An exciting chocolate bestiary appeared in the store each

Christmas, dominated by bears and monkeys and mice and cats, and herded by groups of chocolate Santas. Other – inedible – Christmas specialities bought in by Bilbow, some of which came out year after year, were boxes of marbles containing both plain glass and multicoloured sorts, cards of penknives, silvery repeaters firing long pink strips of caps, torches, paint boxes, watch chains, brightly coloured pinafores and aprons, oilcloth table coverings patterned like draughts boards, red handkerchiefs both plain and with white spots.

The personality and authority of the grocer dilated with his stock, and with the swelling contribution which flowed in for his raffle. This was the highlight of the village festivities, held on Christmas Eve when the shop walls turned elastic, for whereas the little store could comfortably hold a dozen people standing, it had been known to pack in over fifty for the raffle – though this did also include people standing like prisoners at the bar peering over the metal grille at the post-office end and also standing in the little meal annexe, where the all-pervading smell of the fish meal cocktail – some of it past its prime – was a small handicap to enjoyment because of the sneezing it produced.

Last to arrive was the elderly school cleaner, bent and shy, sad, shawled and secretive, walking with difficulty through the snow in

her clogs. She had performed her duty loyally and to the best of her progressively failing strength for a quarter of a century, and the sad saga of her chronically ill-paid service runs through the Managers' Minutes for the whole twenty-five years. Time after time, the Managers had recommended a rise but were always thwarted by the bureaucrats.

The dreary story of injustice dragged on. On 25 August 1941, 'The Chairman stated that the Managers had been summoned to hear and discuss an application from Miss Morgan, the School Caretaker and Cleaner for an increase in wages. Miss Morgan based her application on the facts that during the 22 years she had been employed she had received only one small increase and that having no other source of income she found it impossible to carry on with the present increased cost of living . . .' Finally the ageing spinster decided to give the system victory and on 11 June 1944 the Chairman announced the resignation of Miss M. A. Morgan after nearly twenty-five years as school cleaner.

When the shop opened to Miss Morgan's timid knock that Christmas Eve and she was squeezed in near the door, it was stocked tight as an upright sardine tin and, had anybody been inclined to brood on the fact, about as comfortable, but the presence of the prizes on the counter, the festive chatter which rivalled mattins in the rookery, the coloured paper streamers fluttering and floating on the gale of village breath, produced a growing spirit of Christmas celebration.

The sleeves of his best grey suit, tailored in Bilbow's thinner pre-grocer days, rode up almost to his elbows as he raised his arms to enjoin silence. Placing his hands on the counter edge, he flashed grey dentures.

'Here we are again, people bach,' he began, 'standing by here as the world is spinning into Capricorn, the tenth signature in the Zodiyac. I wonder if that is going to be lucky for those whose birthdays fall into this segiment of the heavens.'

He passed his hands briefly over the prizes, a food hamper, a basket of oranges, apples, bananas, dates and figs, a miniature chest of tea.

He turned to the plain, hook-nosed lady smiling by his side, and said, 'The missus has been the one to play the Lady Bountiful – or should I say Beautiful – this year, and has put up these scrumptious prizes herself. The point now in all our minds is – who is going to win them, whose planet injunctions are going to come together for the bull's-eye, to win this lovely jackpot or perhaps should I say jillpot. He! He! Ho! Ho!'

Bilbow was undoubtedly in process of getting the oracular bit between his dentures. Pausing for a moment, he lifted up his arms as though to bless his audience and, now with a more serious mien, began again with 'I have just been reading the secrets of the Kaboolah . . .' when a man's voice with a tone of impatience and, for those near enough to testify, with the smell of home-brew on his breath, shouted from behind the post office grille, 'Never mind the bloody Beulah, Bilbow, wot about the bloody raffle?'

This was followed immediately by a rib-tingling signal to Bilbow from Aggie's punitive elbow, delivered from long practice so sharply and deftly as to be almost invisible to the audience. The grocer's spell was broken and the same voice now struck up loudly, with unmistakably derisive intention, 'Why are we waiting' followed by 'Count your blessings', and the whole shop joined in, with the exception of Bilbow and Aggie, standing somewhat sheepishly and over-dentured at the counter. They sang it through to the end, when it was followed by cheering, jeering and clapping.

Bilbow lifted his arms again but the meeting was now out of control, until the practical Aggie, with another elbow injunction into her husband's waistcoat, indicated the biscuit tin which contained the names of the ticket holders.

Holding the tin aloft, an act which slowly stilled the tumult, Bilbow began. 'Ladies and gentlemen . . .' only to be interrupted once more by the same voice from the Post Office.

'Never mind the bloody posh stuff, Bilbow, wot about the bloody raffle . . .' which was followed by roars of laughter.

Defeated now, Bilbow took off the lid, placed the tin on the counter, bent down and pulled an upturned vinegar bottle crate into position, so that short-statured Aggie, moving to the podium of honour, suddenly acquired inches. Hook-nosed and smiling, and with her eyes carefully away from the biscuit box, she stirred up the folded names with her right hand, picked one out of the tin, and handed it unopened to John John the roadman, whose diaconal status somehow neutralised any suggestion of chicanery.

Peering through his metal-rimmed glasses, John looked round, just like he did when he announced the next hymn in chapel and said, 'The name of the winner of the first prize is Miss Mary Ann Morgan . . .'

A ragged cheer broke out, with any personal disappointment quickly overtaken by realisation that the school cleaner, one of the poorest people in the village, had won the Christmas food hamper. Second prize went to a village spinster, a close friend of the shopkeeper and his wife, to an accompaniment of loud ironic cheers. The oranges and apples prize went to the blacksmith.

Much to Nana's disgust nothing came the way of the Jones family. She paid her florin dutifully each year but forebore to attend the ceremony on the grounds that it was too common, and invariably another example of the Gwilym Lloyd George 'chick-canary' which distorted the laws of chance and natural justice.

What was to be Bilbow's last village raffle was over, the cheers and counter-cheers given, but loth now to leave the warm festive shop, the crowd continued to chatter and wait as though for a bonus entertainment. From time to time, the voice of Home-brew from behind the post office grille rang out loud and clear in breast and bottom jokes which produced gales of laughter. Then Home-brew began a high light tenor rendering of the Welsh folk songs which everybody present knew, and the choral singing progressed as it always did to favourite hymns.

Then Home-brew raised his arms in the lamplight and calling out, 'Order now by there – order I say', singled out by name his mates in quartet harmony – Elsie the contralto, Myfanwy the blackbird soprano, Telyn who sang the air – and the crowded shop hushed as the four squeezed up close and, with heads together, the deeply Welsh-accented words were enfolded by the warm voices, each part-harmony sung with awareness of the need to mate with the others so that there were not four voices any more but one blended note infinitely lovelier than the sum of the parts. The audience stood as still as figures in a frieze, as the carol swelled,

'We will rock you, rock you, rock you.'

And the singing stilled and gripped the listeners, and the meaning of Christ's birth seemed to come mysteriously alive in the tiny shop, so that after interchange of Christmas greetings, there was no more to be said and the company, including a now moist-eyed Home-brew – who carried the old cleaner's food hamper home – passed silently with serious faces into the snowbound village street and dispersed to the gloaming of their culm-fire homes. And as midnight approached, Abermawr began to roar, the gale swept in from the sea and the school bell once again lulled the sleeping village with ghostly carillons of its own.

MON 14

A lecture on temperance wa[s]
the scholars this morning. [?]
appreciation by loud appl[ause]

Attendance: 4 children a[?]
& Yan Morgan reported to h[?]

Weather: Strong North W[?]
but expected to clear by t[?]

TUES 15

Every child advised that [?]
parents regarding the com[?]
head inspection at half pa[st]

Attendance: Only 2 chil[dren]
Gwylim Thomas of Park[?]
with signs of a rash.

Weather: Much improved [?]
bright sunshine througho[ut]

WED 16

Llewelyn achieves success[?]
Eisteddfod Committee. Mr[?]
this result. The letter com[?]
earliest post.

Attendance: 3 scholars
Morgans' whooping cough